LEAVING IT ALL BEHIND

LEAVING IT ALL BEHIND

←ONE FAMILY'S SEARCH→

MATTHEW S. MAZZA

TOWHEAD INDUSTRIES, LLC
SANTA BARBARA
2014

LEAVING IT ALL BEHIND
Copyright © 2014 Matthew S. Mazza

ISBN 978-0-615-97891-8

First trade paperback edition March 2014

Mr. Mazza is available to speak at your live event (barring scheduling conflicts). Please contact Towhead Industries to discuss any potential opportunities.

Typesetting by Walton Mendelson
www.12on14.com

Towhead Industries, LLC
Santa Barbara, California
(805) 845-1259
www.towheadtravel.com

For my wife and best friend, Wendi, and our two
beautiful daughters, Lily and Kate, the loves of my life.
But for your adventurous spirit and our shared wanderlust,
none of this would have been possible.
And I'd still be just a lawyer.

PROLOGUE

Without deviation from the norm, progress is not possible.
—Frank Zappa

"SHE'S TOO YOUNG."

My wife, Wendi, didn't need to say it. She was referring to our younger daughter, Kate, who was then just three years old. This was an issue we had discussed and considered and debated, *ad nauseum*, over the previous few months.

"I know," I replied plainly, as we had long ago concluded that this was indeed a matter of fact. We had also long ago concluded that our older daughter, Lily, was a perfect age for the long journey ahead. She had turned six a few days earlier.

A deep silence followed for what seemed like an eternity. There was nothing left to say.

I could hear Wendi breathing shallow next to me and thus knew she hadn't fallen back to sleep despite the obscenely early hour. We were in a spare bedroom in her parents' home, in a familiar but still borrowed bed under freshly starched sheets that typically accompany an impermanent accommodation. It dawned on me as we laid together in the cold stillness of the early morning that these would be the sheets with which we would begin to associate home over the coming months. My mind raced in all directions, most light and playful but others shades darker, more troubled.

"It's time," I said, eventually. The clock read 4:30 a.m.

"I know." We quietly got out of bed, dressed quickly, and woke our young daughters, who slipped on the simple clothes we'd laid out for them the night before. We headed for the airport.

And we left life as we knew it behind.

We had no idea that we were leaving it for good.

—•—

We were a happy family back then. I guess I don't know how else to say it. I was a business litigation attorney and had a reasonably successful practice. We lived in a fantastic place in Santa Barbara, California. Wendi stayed home with Lily and Kate, and was a great mother and wife and friend. The girls were cute and funny and eager to learn and engaged and social with near-constant play dates and lessons and practices and all the other *accoutrements* of day-to-day life in modern California. Between it all, we ran around like crazed lunatics from school auctions to dinners with friends to beach parties to whatever else was going on over any given weekend. We had fun—a lot of fun—but it was at a bewilderingly frenetic pace.

Don't get me wrong, I'm not complaining. Our life was terrific by most objective measures, a cookie-cutter example of two pretty darn middle-class kids doing pretty darn well. Looking back, I now see that we followed a quite conventional path—college and graduate degrees, a prestigious job at a great firm, two beautiful daughters, a Labrador Retriever, a Volvo Wagon, 401(k)s and IRAs and 529 Plans—despite never really intending to do so. We even whispered to each other about it sometimes, after one too many glasses of wine over dinner with friends or late at night in bed before we'd fall asleep. "It's funny that after all these years we've got what we always said we wanted," we'd say. "Who knew?" And then we'd pour another glass of wine or exchange a goodnight kiss and fall asleep.

Here's the thing: We *did* have what we always wanted. We had exactly what everyone always said we *should* want. We had exactly what financial advisors and life insurance agents and career counselors advised was appropriate and reasonable. We painted by numbers, we checked the boxes, we did it all right. We succeeded.

And we were happy back then, even *very* happy.

But somewhere along the line, something changed. It's hard to put my finger on when, exactly, it happened, but looking back it is clear that something changed.

We changed.

We didn't start loving each other or the kids any less, and our relationship remained strong (like it pretty much always has been). But the dialogue between us—the language we used to describe our day-to-day reality—began to change. And that was the beginning of the end of life as we knew it.

I became less thrilled (understatement of the year, by the way) with the idea of litigating for the rest of my working life. We started questioning the rationale behind many things we had always taken for granted. (Why do the kids need constant classes and practices and activities? Why should I work a job I don't love for forty years so that we can have big bank accounts and play bad golf in a stiflingly boring retirement? Why shouldn't we pursue our passions relentlessly? Etc.) We questioned most everything about our life, and some of the answers we found surprised us. Ultimately, I think we found ourselves feeling constrained by the very existence we had so carefully constructed.

Looking back through the lens of hindsight with the clarity that comes when all the noise, all the stress and all the *angst*, that stems from the hustle and bustle of daily life fades to black, I recognize now that we both wanted the same thing: Some uninterrupted time away. Time away from a demanding career and constantly buzzing blackberry. Time away from a rigid schedule of swimming lessons and ballet classes and soccer practices and gymnastics and tennis lessons and even school (yeah, I said it). Time away together.

As a family.

Looking back through that same lens I see that we were all a bit burnt out, maybe, and ready for something a little different, something a little ... *adventurous*.

So we made a decision. Unbeknownst to us, it was a life-changing decision, made innocently enough during a simple conversation between Wendi and me about life and kids and happiness over an otherwise unremarkable lunch on one otherwise ordinary autumn day in Santa Barbara.

"What if we actually did it?" Wendi (mischievously) asked, biting into her typically healthy salad.

"Did what?" I countered, oblivious to her overtures, mouth full of tuna sandwich with extra mayo.

"You know, took some time off and traveled around the world with the kids, like we've talked about."

I stopped chewing.

We spent the ensuing seven months planning and plotting and sometimes perspiring, and we eventually came up with the beginnings of a trip that provided both for the uninterrupted time away we craved as well as for a real diversity of experience that we thought would keep the girls (and us) interested and having fun. We met with schoolteachers—Lily, then five, was in Kindergarten, and Kate, then three, was a preschooler—and travel doctors and grandparents. We got cold feet (*i.e.*, "this is crazy, we are definitely not going") and hot feet (*i.e.*, "this is the opportunity of a lifetime and we should leave today"). We bought backpacks and water sterilization devices and baggage scales and pocketknives. Eventually, we bought plane tickets, and our fate was sealed.

I closed my law practice. We moved out of our house after the girls finished the school year. What we couldn't fit into a single POD, we donated or gave to friends or (gasp) trashed. We stuffed two large packs full with clothes and electronics and other things we believed a family may need at one point or another on an indefinite and largely undefined trip around the world. We packed one small backpack with games and art supplies and books for the girls. We threw in one of my old, beat up acoustic guitars at the last minute.

And we got on an airplane.

The truth is that it wasn't as hard as you might think. Many of the "serious concerns" we had before we hit the road ultimately proved quite trivial, and the challenges we expected were less, well, *challenging*. We had our difficulties, to be sure—there was that zip line accident in France and that incredibly wrong turn in South Africa...oh, and there was that terrifying moment when we lost Kate near the *Grand Canal* in Venice and that wild night in Kathmandu (and another on the *Mekong River* near Luang Prabang)—but the simple fact is that our time on the road was the very best of my life. Period.

One of our pre-departure "serious concerns" was that Lily and Kate might not remember everything we did. (I'll say at the outset that this proved perhaps the silliest "concern," as the time we spent together on the road was truly formative in every sense of the word; it quite clearly shaped our daughters' lives, personalities and thinking, and generally permeated their very being.) So we decided to keep a multi-media journal of our travels to share with them when they got older. As we developed that idea, we realized that we could also share our experience with family and friends, who were interested—quite interested indeed—in our (irresponsible and financially reckless) endeavor.

So we asked a friend to build a simple website, and I wrote a blog about our experience. (Wendi laboriously reviewed and edited my often impulsive prose, so thank her for what I see as relative literary balance.) We both took pictures and videos too, and at least some of them found their way into our posts.

Fortunately, life is inherently unpredictable and the website soon grew beyond our family and immediate friends, something we never anticipated. I was offered a column at a weekly newspaper in Santa Barbara (unanticipated again). Articles were published. People read them.

Things developed from there.

And now, when I sit and look back over the words that follow, the words I wrote as we moved through time and space together, I am struck by what we accomplished as a family. It brings me to tears, still, and I hope you'll see—not just in my written ramblings but also between the lines themselves—what I see clearly, even now.

I see a family, together, throwing caution and worry and other bullshit to the wind in an effort to scratch the surface and find something else, maybe even something more. I see inspiration and passion and understanding. I see an unbreakable connection that will bond me to my wife and kids forever.

I see peace, man. I see love.

Perhaps most importantly, though, I see that we were all genuinely happy—under anybody's definition—sharing time and experience and life together. Nobody can ever take that away from us.

Santa Barbara, California
United States of America
November 2013

PART ONE

BREAKING AWAY

"The problem is all inside your head," she said to me;
"The answer is easy if you take it logically.
I'd like to help you in your struggle to be free.
There must be fifty ways to leave your lover."
                                        —Paul Simon

CHAPTER 1
THOUGHTS ON FATHER'S DAY

Montclair, New Jersey
United States of America
June 2011

If the new American father feels bewildered and even defeated,
let him take comfort from the fact that whatever he does in any
fathering situation has a fifty percent chance of being right.
—Bill Cosby

I VAGUELY RECALL SPENDING FATHER'S DAY 2009 in the same way I spent many Father's Days since my first daughter's birth. I went to the beach, I tossed horseshoes, I drank beer, I laughed with friends. It was undeniably fun and likely even deserved. But despite the fact that my family was there with me, I took the day for myself in many ways, choosing to spend as much time "relaxing" as I did with my daughters. Perhaps that is why I only vaguely remember it.

Seven months ago, my wife and I decided to travel around the world with our daughters. We thought it would teach them something important about the human condition, and we wanted to show them and ourselves the far corners of the globe. Ultimately, we wanted to spend some uninterrupted time together as a family.

Only now are we beginning to truly understand that we didn't know much beyond that. Only now, I think, do we see the full range of possibilities that may stem from our decision.

Lily is six. Kate is three. We've moved out of our home in Santa Barbara, California. I've closed down my law practice and stopped earning income. We've pulled the girls out of school. We've packed all of our worldly possessions—save those we can carry on our backs—into a single Portable On Demand Storage container. We've gotten rid of the rest one way (*e.g.*, donated) or another (*e.g.*, trashed).

Perhaps most surprisingly, however, is the fact that we've done all of this *intentionally*. We've weighed pros and cons. We've analyzed benefits and detriments. We've exercised free will and, whether "rightly" or "wrongly," we've chosen this path.

We accept fully the consequences of our decisions, both positive and negative, whatever they may be.

At the end of the day, we (firmly) believe that there is something important to all of this. We believe that spending time, *this* time, together as a family is invaluable. We believe that taking a moment away from the smartphone and the regimented schedule of conventional California life (think work and school and swimming lessons and ballet classes, etc.) to reflect upon our past, present and future is good.

And yet now, as we begin our travels after months of planning and plotting and talking and thinking, it seems that nothing is really certain. From where we will go to when we'll come home and what we'll do when we get there. From how we will adapt to our newfound lifestyle as vagabond parents and gypsy spouses to how our kids will act as world citizens. From what each of us may ultimately get out of this to what each of us may not. These are uncertain times. Uncertain times indeed.

Uncertainty, be damned.

We fully intend to see the world together, sometimes through the eyes of our kids and sometimes through our own. We'll volunteer and, occasionally, accept the charity of others. We'll live in everything from farmhouses and orphanages to boats and shacks. We'll employ every imaginable mode of transportation (and then some). We'll take life as it comes, moment by moment, day by day. And we'll do it together. In good times and bad. In sickness and health.

And we'll let the chips fall where they may.

———•———

We left California on June 18, 2011, in a generally eastward direction. I spent June 19, 2011—Father's Day—with my wife and kids (and delightful aunt and uncle) in New York. We saw *Mary Poppins* on Broadway, walked through *Times Square* and climbed to the top of the *Empire State Building* at sunset. It was fun. *Really* fun.

As we stood on the 86th floor observation deck and looked out over Manhattan, Lily whispered in my ear, "I can see the whole world from here, Daddy."

"Almost," I told her, "but just wait."

Now that's a Father's Day I won't forget as long as I live.

CHAPTER 2
A PERFECT PINT

Dublin, Ireland
July 2011

Blood is thicker than Guinness.
—English Proverb (adapted)

HORDES FLOCK TO DUBLIN each year in search of an elusive bounty. Some make the pilgrimage to the *Guinness Storehouse* at *St. James's Gate*—a truly religious experience for many—and stroll the streets and alleys of *Temple Bar*. Others pay for pub crawls ostensibly to see the favorite watering holes of Joyce and Yeats and Wilde and Swift. But they all hunt for the same treasure.

The Perfect Pint.

I found my perfect pint on Chatham Street, in a relatively quiet place just off of bustling Grafton Street. And I found it without even really trying.

Traveling with my wife and two young daughters presents certain, ah, *limitations*. Had I been traveling alone, I may have devoted more time to the hunt. But Lily and Kate (and Wendi) can stand only so many drunken tourists and pubs so it was not to be. Instead, we spent five days exploring Dublin (we even took the Viking Tour!), meeting other kids and parents in many of the fantastic local parks (*St. Stephens Green* and *Iveagh Gardens* were real favorites) and otherwise getting to know the place.

Dublin is a terrific spot and we—kids included—had a blast. The whole city center area is vibrant and very walkable, which, to me, is a key quality in a city. We were literally able to stroll out our door and find great food and myriad sites (everything from *St. Patrick's Cathedral* to *Trinity College* to *Merrion Square*) within relatively few steps (even for Kate). I went for a short but sweet run (ok, slow jog) along the *River Liffey*—fondly referred to as the *Sniffy Liffey* due to its well-known odoriferous qualities—early one morning and ended up exploring *Phoenix Park*. Two different people stopped me to see if I needed directions; I guess they don't see too many foreign runners (ok, slow joggers) at 6:30am on Sunday morning. Great people, great place.

But I digress. It rained on Friday so we donned our foul weather gear and braved the elements, expecting the city to slow down given the inclement weather. We found instead that the streets and restaurants and shops had really come alive. Dubliners and tourists alike moved quickly through crowded alleys, laughing and talking without regard for the rain or cold. (Quite a change from Santa Barbara.) We followed suit and made it to our appointment on Chatham Street a few minutes early.

We had arranged a meeting with my distant but super welcoming and hospitable Irish relatives, whom I'd neither met nor even heard of in any meaningful fashion until just a few weeks prior. We sat in their pub, *Sheehans*, which they've owned for nearly 80 years and talked and laughed like old friends.

Maureen is my grandfather's cousin and she grew up in the flat above the place. Alana is her niece and now runs the pub with her brother Paul. We looked through an album of old pictures of my grandfather and his siblings and others that I had never seen. We ate hot Irish Stew (simple and delicious, especially on a cold and wet day) and the kids had fish and chips. I had a pint of Guinness.

Oh ok, all right.

I had *two* pints of Guinness.

When it was time to leave, Alana forced an umbrella on us and sent us on our way to a great place for a sweet snack and coffee. Then we hit the park at *St. Stephens Green* and played in the rain before heading back to the apartment for the night. Great day.

It turns out, for me, anyway, that a "perfect" pint is just as much about the circumstances in which you drink it as it is about how it is poured or when it was brewed. For me, perfection was drinking *those* pints with *those* people and *that* stew in *that* pub on *that* day in Dublin.

I couldn't imagine it any other way.

(For the record, I did eventually break away and hit *St. James's Gate*. They pour a pretty damn good pint there, too.)

CHAPTER 3
INTERNATIONAL MAN OF MISERY

Balleydehob, Ireland
July 2011

I never have more than one drink before dinner.
But I do like that one to be large and very strong
and very cold, and very well made.
—James Bond

WE LEFT DUBLIN on a Tuesday, headed for a small and secluded farmhouse near Balleydehob, a town fairly deep in west County Cork. Before that, though, I left Wendi and the girls in our apartment near *Christ Church Cathedral* and went alone to the airport to pick up the rental car that would carry us there.

As a rule, I generally don't like to reveal too much about myself in writing, but I think it's safe to say here that I'm no "car guy" and frankly couldn't possibly care less about what I drive or the side on which the steering wheel happens to fall. But when I got behind the wheel of that (beautiful) French rental car and zipped my way back into Dublin, the feeling was unmistakable. It started deep in my loins and spread quickly throughout my mind and body and soul.

I felt like James Bond. *James frickin' Bond*, man.

I zipped and whirred my way through traffic, driving (quite dangerously, I might add) at high speeds from the wrong side of the car and the road down city streets and alleys. I ripped through the gears of the manual Citroen, exploiting its small stature and nimbleness at every opportunity. I broke a few speed limits. I (nearly) ran a few red lights. Loud Irish music poured from the radio. I eluded capture by foreign spy agencies.

I also lost track of time.

When I (finally) got back to the apartment, Wendi had already moved all the bags downstairs and was waiting (im)patiently with the girls in the lobby. I quickly loaded everything into the tiny car—my guitar was wedged between the driver's and passenger's seats and backpacks were perched precariously above the girls' heads on the small shelf above the purported "trunk space" in the rear—and we took off, slowly and responsibly at first.

But, alas, I am what I am. Even despite the absurdly overloaded car and the fact that my two young, precious daughters were without car seats or boosters or any other reasonably crafted child protective devices, I was unable to completely let go of my covert international assignment.

We rocketed through the *Wicklow Mountains*—kids giggling, Wendi glaring (only to avoid showing her true enjoyment, I think)—stopping only for food and wine (just one glass, don't worry) in a quaint town in the Irish countryside. From there, we blasted onto the gorgeous winding country roads that would lead us to our farmhouse hidden amongst the beautiful wildflowers and rolling greens of west Cork. The Citroen purred and took corners like it was on rails. I was considering stopping for a pair of driving gloves and a five-point harness.

Then Kate projectile vomited all over the backseat.

Now "vomit" is by no means a word I use lightly. When

I say "vomit," I mean VOMIT. Big deal for all involved. Lily instantly began crying and effectively clawing at her window. Wendi mopped and comforted. No longer feeling quite like Mr. Bond, I pulled off, gently, at the first opportunity.

When one packs bags for an extended period of travel through many areas of the world, one has many items at one's disposal. Malaria pills, check. Diarrhea medicine, no problem. Military-grade wound dressings, child's play. But one can't always foresee each nuance of the future and we neither planned nor packed for VOMIT CLEAN-UP. Supplies were limited or non-existent.

Serendipitously, though, we had pulled off the road into the parking lot of a fairly remote pub. (I don't know that it even had a name.) It wasn't exactly the most welcoming pub we'd come across in Ireland but we needed help, fast, so Lily and I walked cautiously through the worn doors.

The place was empty except for three old hardened Irish men in a corner having a whiskey and a spirited discussion about something in Gaelic. Traditional music played on an old radio. The bartender turned and stared at us. The old men stopped talking and did the same. Lily scaled a barstool. I felt, um, *uneasy*, and apologetically explained our predicament.

The bartender soon smiled wide and offered hot water, towels and various sterilization-related products. The trio of old men laughed and offered their condolences before going back to their whiskeys and conversation. And when the bartender brought the promised supplies, she offered me (and maybe even Lily) a pint.

It was then that I knew I would love west Cork.

I mean, where else in the world can you share a truly authentic moment with your six-year-old daughter over a properly poured Guinness with a hospitable Irish bartender and lively Irish music—interrupted occasionally by Gaelic outbursts from a group of friendly Irish drunkards—playing softly in the background?

We took our time, cleaned up, dusted ourselves off and jumped back in the Citroen. We took the rest of the drive—only about another hour—slowly, wandering the Irish countryside on paved and then dirt roads until we reached our destination just before sunset. It was quite a drive even after we slowed down a bit, stunning beauty surrounded us everywhere and we took the time to appreciate it and chat about it with the kids.

Ultimately, that's what this whole thing is all about: Slowing down and sharing time and experience together for a while. At this particular moment, it's also about figuring out how best to rid the Citroen of a lingering sour stench so we can cruise comfortably out to the coast in a day or two.

Sorry Kate. I promise I'll take it easy on the whole international spy driving thingy going forward.

Mommy's already taken the keys away from me anyway.

CHAPTER 4
LILY THE LINGUIST: "PISSED AS A NOSE"

Belfast, Northern Ireland
July 2011

We don't need no education.
—Pink Floyd

I THOUGHT I'D GO AHEAD and share this "travel-related learning experience" now, even though we are moving pretty quickly through Belfast, Northern Ireland, *en route* to Stranraer, Scotland. Nomadic homeschooling is not always what you might expect.

Relevant Circumstantial Evidence: We were on a train from Dublin to Belfast when a rather large man stepped directly on my foot. He was holding a 24-ounce Budweiser can, and traveling with his wife and children. He apologized profusely and told me that he thought my foot was a "lump in the carpet" (this prompted him to laugh hysterically).

Twenty minutes later, the very same large man walked by again, this time holding a 24-ounce Budweiser *Light* can. He stopped and asked all about our family and the trip. His words were slurred, at best, and every time he opened his mouth to talk, Wendi and I braced ourselves for the record-setting string of (sometimes quite vulgar) profanities that came as part of his otherwise appropriate questions and comments.

I ribbed him for drinking the King of Beers in Ireland. More laughing. More jovial profane outbursts.

After a few minutes of friendly conversation, he leaned in close to me and belched forth, "I'M PISSED AS A NOSE" before staggering off. Nice guy.

(We watched him guzzle what was left of the can when the train stopped. Then he hugged at least one Irish Rail employee before helping his kid into a stroller and wandering off with family in tow.)

Translation: Lily the Linguist watched the whole scene unfold with keen interest. When I asked her to translate "PISSED AS A NOSE," she responded confidently: "He was telling us that he was PERFECT, Daddy."

Accuracy: Depends on your perspective. If you see our friend as "the happiest guy on the train," then the Linguist did pretty darn well. If you instead see him as "a raging alcoholic who was neglecting his wife and children," then she was a bit off.

After-Acquired Information: We learned after telling this story to a couple Scots that the phrase was likely "PISSED AS A NEWT." We're not sure how that might change the Linguist's translation—indeed, I'm not sure I totally understand the phrase in the first place (do newts even drink?)—but we've decided not to ask her again in the interest of good (well, *better*) parenting.

CHAPTER 5
ON IRELAND AND SCOTLAND
(OR DADDY ALMOST RUINED OUR TRIP)

Paris, France
July 2011

I get by with a little help from my friends.
—The Beatles

WE'VE BEEN IN PARIS FOR A FEW DAYS NOW and have a great apartment in the 7th Arrondissement. We are really enjoying the City of Light, but that is a topic for another day.

The apartment has allowed us some quiet, relaxing time in the mornings and evenings and I've been thinking a lot about what we consider the first leg of our trip, Ireland and Scotland. The truth is that it was great, and many of the concerns we had before leaving now seem rather trivial. Lily and Kate have proven wonderful little travelers and they are excited and engaged. Seeing new places and meeting new people with them has been pretty easy, maybe even easier than if Wendi and I were on our own. Most people (though not all) are enchanted by them and that opens many doors.

With that said, the first few weeks of our trip have also seen a number of blunders (or worse). We are still figuring out just how this will work and there has been a steep learning curve. But, call it fate or karma or good fortune or even luck, we have escaped relatively unscathed (except for maybe an occasionally bruised ego). Many kind folks have already stepped up and lent helping hands as we have needed them and that has made a hugely positive impact on our experience. We owe each a debt of gratitude.

So then, what, exactly, has transpired since Kate's sudden "illness" outside Balleydehob?

A lot, actually.

And it ain't all good.

Blissed-Out in Balleydehob

It turned out that we all loved west Cork and the "farmhouse." *Mt. Kid Cottage* is a fairly rustic little place set way back off a highway through a labyrinth of one-lane county roads. ("Rustic" is not entirely accurate, I guess... there is a hot tub and a dry sauna to ensure proper mood.) It is a beautiful place without too many people. (Think west Marin County meets Bodega Bay or Sea Ranch in California.) All of us loved the big grassy fields and grazing cows and laid back vibe. Small towns with names like Schull and Skibbereen are scattered around and we visited many of them. We also drove out to *Mizen Head*, which is the furthest southwest point of the Emerald Isle and a visually stunning place. There is a fantastic beach at *Barley Cove* that we also loved (felt a little like home except the water is bright green and chilly).

We cooked a few delicious meals in the Cottage with local fish and produce and drank French wines (in the Irish countryside!). The kids played in the pastures and hot tub. We took turns in the sauna. We played a zillion games. We watched *The Sound of Music* twice, and fancied ourselves like the *von Trapps*. (We all still have a good laugh when Kate bursts into *"Doe, a Deer, a female Deer...,"* which happens nearly as often as the *Mary Poppins* medley she nails.) We had a great time, a memorable one. Even if we didn't actually do much of anything the whole time we were there.

Broke in Belfast

We left the Cottage on a Sunday—choosing the motorway rather than country roads to avoid any "issues" with Kate—to return the rental car in Dublin and then catch a train for Belfast. It was a fairly uneventful trip (except for that whole "Pissed as a Nose" exchange).

With that said, we did indeed have a problem that had been building since we landed in Ireland. The new ATM card we brought with us had not been working and the only way we could get cash was to go into a particular bank and do a whole song and dance with passports and pleading and pinky-swears. That had worked fine for Dublin and Balleydehob, but Belfast doesn't operate on the Euro, it uses the British Pound and has different rules. We knew this, of course, but had no (easy) way to get Pounds in Ireland. And no banks or money exchangers are open in Northern Ireland on a Sunday afternoon.

So let's just say that we arrived in Belfast "cash poor."

We needed a cab from the train station in central Belfast to *Camera House*, our bed and breakfast. Cabs don't take credit cards in Belfast.

So, again, we pleaded and pinky-swore. We showed the cab driver our (tired, hungry) children. He politely refused to leave the train station. So we offered him 50 Euros for a 10 Pound cab-ride. We sped away.

When we arrived at *Camera House*, I explained our predicament (*i.e.*, begged and pleaded) and the proprietor immediately lent us the money to pay the cab fare in Pounds. I'm not sure how many places in Santa Barbara would have done something like that for a family of exhausted foreigners so quickly. The bottom line is that *Camera House* consistently bent over backwards for us while we were there, and made our 36-hour stay, well, *easy*.

Equally good was the fact that *Camera House* is located near *Queen's College* and there is a fair amount to do within walking distance. We spent the next day exploring the *Botanic Gardens Park* and the *Ulster Museum*, which really caters to kids. We had a huge milkshake at *Maggie May's* and a great dinner outside but under warm blankets at *The Barking Dog* (budget be damned!). The whole thing was a blast, even if only a day or two.

Short and sweet.

Easy Living in Edinburgh

From Belfast, we took a ferry across the Irish Sea to Stranraer, Scotland, where we picked up another car and drove three hours across the country to Edinburgh. (No vomiting!) We stayed a few nights with some new friends in Dunbar, a small community—and John Muir's birthplace—on Scotland's east coast.

First of all, our Scot friends are wonderful people. They spent just over a year canvassing the world with their kids and are a fountain of knowledge about extended family travel. (We met them online as we researched our trip, and they actually stopped by our home in Santa Barbara for lunch while they were traveling in California before we left.) They also opened their home to and took good care of us, bringing us to a great park for the girls, making us meals and acting as tour guides in Edinburgh. They basically took a fair amount of time out of their lives and careers to ensure that we had a great experience in eastern Scotland.

And we did. There's perhaps no better way to see a place than with a friendly bunch who knows it well. (We'll have to remember that going forward.)

Edinburgh is a wonderful city. We climbed to the top of the *Scott Monument*, and the girls loved the narrow spiraling staircases and view from the top. In fact, that experience started a new thing for us: Lily and Kate want to go to the "tippy" of every damn monument in Europe. We visited the castle, had lunch at *The Elephant House* (Harry Potter was born there!), saw a show involving swords and shields and maces and other maiming implements put on by (alleged) *Scottish Highlanders*, rolled around on the hills and lawns of *Princes Street Gardens*, shed a tear for *Greyfriars Bobby* and otherwise generally enjoyed ourselves.

Again, a blast.

Searching for Nessie in Loch Ness

We packed up and left our friends and Dunbar, a great coastal town in its own right (the salty breeze coming off the North Sea and *Firth of Forth* reminded us a bit of home), for the *Scottish Highlands* and, in particular, Inverness and Loch Ness. We were on the hunt for the *Loch Ness Monster* (aka "Nessie") and the girls were thrilled.

We hadn't expected much out of Inverness itself, and thought of it more as a launching point for a search expedition. But it turned out to be a fun city and we had a good experience (except for the "gentleman" running a highly recommended dining establishment who treated us so badly and with such disdain that we got up and left, thank you very much, in favor of a new Jamaican place down the street that not only made a mean jerk chicken but also gave proper respect to Bob Marley).

We hit a cool little pizza joint another night and stumbled upon a show of highland dancers and pipe bands put on by local school kids and their elders in an ancient Irish courtyard. The girls have quickly developed a love of bagpipes and kilts so you can imagine how this went over; there was much laughing and dancing and general merrymaking. We got home late and slept well.

Loch Ness is sort of what you might expect, but it was a huge hit for us. Lily and Kate devoured scientific data about the huge body of water at the *Loch Ness Centre & Exhibition* and we took a boat ride aboard the *Nessie Hunter*. (Homeschool!) I think we saw the beast at least fifty times.

Most important, ironically, was that we stayed at *Glenuig House*, a great little bed and breakfast that made Inverness very accessible. The breakfasts were delicious, the room was comfortable and we were just a few short blocks from the *River Ness*. Perfect. But it was our introduction to the proprietor, Roz, that proved truly invaluable. (And, if you are still awake and can muster three more minutes of reading, then you will know why.)

It is also noteworthy that we resolved our ATM problem— which was worse than we initially thought—while we were in Inverness. By we, of course, I mean a young, creative banker in Santa Barbara who went far out of his way to bend a few rules and really help us out, and we owe him (more than) one. Seriously.

High in Skye

Beinn Edra House, in Valtos, Isle of Skye, was our last stop in Scotland. The drive to Skye alone was amazing and the island itself is a truly visually stunning place. It's hard to describe it in any meaningful fashion, frankly. Boundless cliffs and ancient rock formations and gorgeous beaches and wild waterfalls and endless fields and sheep and sunsets and skylines and and and…. We were able to relax at *Beinn Edra* (similar to *Mt. Kid Cottage* back in Cork in terms of vibe), which was good. We all loved *Kilt Rock* and *Staffin Bay* (cool beach), and the *Queraing* was great.

Skye is an incredible place.

But perhaps most important was the fact that *Beinn Edra* was run by a couple great people (the Scots referred to at the end of *Lily the Linguist: "Pissed as a Nose"*). They built the main house from the ground up and are working on one or two more on the same property. Very cool. They have two daughters (amongst other older kids) who are five and seven, perfectly aged for Lily and Kate. The foursome were quick friends and spent hours and hours together jumping on a trampoline, making up games and doing all the other things little girls do. (They are keeping in touch and we hope to have them over in California one day.)

Also very cool.

The family at *Beinn Edra* brought us into their house and their world out on Skye and we had a great time. They even took Lily for a walk in the woods and hunted for pinecones while Wendi, Kate and I went into *Portree* for ice cream. All of this felt really good for the kids and we are glad it happened. Thanks *Beinn Edra*!

Oh, I almost forgot to mention the other reason that Wendi, Kate and I went into *Portree* while Lily hunted for pinecones: We had to pick up our passports, credit cards, drivers licenses and other extremely valuable materials from a total and complete stranger.

Yeah, you read that right.

I had left our most important bag—the coveted "black

bag"—containing all necessary travel materials hanging off of my chair at breakfast when we left Inverness for Skye.

Big deal. Huge mistake.

When we discovered that everything—*everything*—had been left (except for one card in my wallet), I just about lost my mind. In fact, but for an email from Roz at *Glenuig House*, we may not have known of my gaffe until we arrived at the Glasgow airport bound for Paris.

Wonder where I was at mentally after learning of my mistake? Think Jack Nicholson in *The Pledge* or *One Flew Over the Cuckoo's Nest* (post-lobotomy).

Without passports, we wouldn't have been able to leave Scotland for France, so our flight, apartment in Paris and houseboat reservation may have been lost. This represents a fair sum of dollars and, just as importantly, a fair amount of time, so it would have been bad. (Read "catastrophic." Especially this early in the trip.)

Even after we received Roz's email, I still was facing a six-hour (minimum) drive back to Inverness, stranding Wendi and the girls at *Beinn Edra House* while I was gone and missing much of what Skye has to offer. (Unless, of course, I drove the winding, precarious, unfamiliar and sometimes one-lane roads all night at Bond-like speeds. Hmmmm...attractive. But still not particularly good. I digress. Again.)

Ultimately, Roz saved our collective behind (and thus, in the process, mine). It was Sunday (again) so no couriers were available but Roz suggested putting our stuff in a package on a bus bound from Inverness for Skye. I was skeptical at first. (All mandatory travel docs and credit cards and extra Euros on some bus in northwest Scotland? That's not in any guidebooks. Rick Steves would not approve.) But Roz and *Beinn Edra* made us comfortable and we put our trip in the hands of complete and total strangers just three weeks after it had begun.

Lo and behold, the bus showed up on time and the package was delivered, intact. No charge, just a smiling bus driver. And a smiling Matt. And a happy family. And a disaster averted.

All because of the kindness of strangers.

We left Skye for Glasgow and spent the night in a cheap hotel. We found an indoor mini-golf course nearby and played eighteen in honor of the rain soaked Scottish Open. The next morning, we flew out of Glasgow and landed in Paris.

No harm, no foul.

One thing is clear, however: I will never leave that damned black bag ever again. Seriously.

That's it. Now we are in Paris, a little wiser for the wear and a little more prepared for the challenges that lay ahead. We are a traveling family and have taken a few lumps, but we've bounced back and are alive and well. It is (very) clear that we will need a hand every now and then, and the Irish and Scots were there for us when we needed them. It was a great introduction to our new lifestyle and we will return the favors one day.

Mark my words.

CHAPTER 6
A BOTCHED KIDNAPPING IN PARIS

Paris, France
July 2011

I like Paris. My problem is I don't like Parisians.
—Sir Lawrence Olivier

WE SPENT A RECENT AFTERNOON exploring the *Musee d'Orsay*, a great museum that has an impressive collection and at least acknowledges children and offers free strollers. (It is also really close to our place and thus we had an escape plan if all hell broke loose.) We saw works by *Monet*, *Van Gogh* and *Cezanne*, amongst others, as well as a wonderful *Manet* exhibit that was really worth the time and effort.

The girls were (mostly) interested, and we must have played two dozen rounds of "I spy, with my little eye." Wendi and I secretly used the game in an effort to focus them on important pieces but, as many parents might imagine, Lily and Kate quickly turned to the old "I spy a booty" or "I spy boobs" while laughing hysterically.

At least they saw some sculptures.

We left the museum as it closed and there were hordes of weary art appreciators wandering aimlessly about. We were weary too and thought it best to have a seat on the front stairs and plan our next move. But then people started sitting down all around us, and a street performance suddenly materialized in the alley right before our eyes.

The whole thing started with a man playing a very casual, meandering tune on an old clarinet that could perhaps best be described as the soundtrack to a "lazy Parisian afternoon strolling along the *Seine*." The girls' attention was focused on a series of colorful cones that had been set up in a long line down the alley, just in front of the man playing clarinet. They were guessing what the cones were for when a younger man in large headphones came flying down the alley on roller skates at breakneck speed without warning, weaving through the cones on one foot while simultaneously spinning around in circles with his second foot in his hand, much like a deranged professional ice skater without the glittery costume.

The crowd went wild. He was going dangerously fast, for sure, and was clearly skilled enough to dodge unsuspecting tourists walking hand-in-hand and not paying attention to anything beyond the gorgeous storefronts tempting passersby with brightly colored meringues and macaroons and other French delights.

Just when the alley became clogged enough with people that it seemed the show was doomed, a third performer—a wild-haired and rather crazy old man—materialized out of nowhere and began heckling those who didn't get out of the way. He'd block their path and stand there, waiting for them to try to get around him only to block them again (and again, and again). He mimicked funny walks, teased bald men about their lack of hair and generally harrassed unsuspecting kids and foreigners relentlessly, all without ever saying a word.

Lily and Kate loved it. (To be fair, so did we.) And it went on for some time, with the clarinet player playing nonchalantly, the skater making pass after more death-defying pass and the certifiably insane guy silently jeering passersby to the delight of the now giant crowd. (Truth be told, Kate was initially very concerned about the heckler—afraid he'd come after us—but she ultimately found him absolutely hilarious). It was quite a show and got better and better as the audience grew and grew.

Then, again without any warning whatsoever, the skater skated right over to us, made a quick motion toward Lily, and then swept her off of the stairs and rode away, fast, with my precious-brilliant-wonderful six-year-old daughter in his arms. There was no time to object.

Concerned is one word that comes to mind as I write. Yes, I think that's quite accurate. *Paralyzed*—yep, *paralyzed*—is another.

You get the idea.

The crowd roared (not an exaggeration) its approval as they skated around the corner and out of sight. An eternity passed as Wendi and I painted toothy smiles on to our faces so the hordes could see how much we were enjoying the fact that our daughter had just completely disappeared with some Parisian street performer. Kate must've asked us where Lily had gone two-hundred times before she suddenly reappeared in the skater's arms.

You'd think we'd have been relieved to see her.

And you'd be wrong.

This was apparently the skater's *piece de resistance*, and the velocity with which he entered the alley was alarming. (There were, in fact, a couple gasps from the crowd. I thought one had come from Wendi but she had long ago lost all ability to utter sound. In fact, she was still grinning like a lunatic.) The ensuing events happened in slow motion; you just have to picture a raucous crowd going absolutely bonkers as Wendi, Kate and I sat still, eyes glued to Lily, who was flying by us, literally in a blur, in the arms of a roller skating dare-devil maniac. I only really remember one thing.

Lily was smiling.

That's right, my sometimes shy, often careful, always cautious kid was quite clearly having a blast doing the single most dangerous thing she'd done in her life. Ever.

No, our first-born daughter did not almost die that day. But when that dude picked her up and skated away toward the *Seine*, Wendi and I had an unspoken moment of genuine terror, during which both of us simultaneously imagined that our eldest child was obviously being stolen from us by a band of deranged Parisian maniacs who ostensibly make their living busking but actually are up to far more devious and despicable dealings.

Alas, she was returned to us, unharmed, much to the delight of the crowd. The show was over. Lily absolutely glowed for the rest of the day.

And so happy (relieved?) were we that all was well and good in the world that we spent the next couple hours sipping rich dark coffees and nibbling those sinful meringues and macaroons in that alley, which, coincidentally, perhaps, we later discovered was just off of a very aptly named *Rue de Lille*.

Ain't life grand?

CHAPTER 7
THE ROTISSERIE CHICKEN INCIDENT

Paris, France
July 2011

Winner, winner; chicken dinner.
—Unknown

I'VE LIVED IN EUROPE TWICE as an exchange student. I spent over four months in Madrid when I was sixteen, and then Wendi and I lived in Barcelona for nearly five months while I was in graduate school. It is probably not surprising, then, that I have seen and experienced a decent portion of Western Europe and generally feel comfortable and confident that I have a reasonable understanding of what's going on here.

But my confidence was shaken yesterday.

By a rotisserie chicken.

We spent the morning relaxing around the apartment after a four day site-seeing blitz that had left us all nearly catatonic. Then we went for the crown: A trip to the "tippy" of the *Eiffel Tower*. The girls had been talking about it all week—especially after studying the height and grandeur of the tower for hours as we waited on the *Champ de Mars* for a dazzling fireworks display on *Bastille Day*—and were effectively vibrating with excitement. The experience lived up to the hype, I think, although Kate wanted to head down after about ten minutes up top.

We thought we'd eat a healthy meal in and try to save some money since France has been a bit hard on the "budget" that we are all too frequently ignoring. I was also excited to cook, and couldn't wait to get into the beautiful markets and butchers shops on our street to handpick perfect French ingredients. I was to go alone, *sans* children, to get some vegetables and meat and make it happen.

I started well with fresh green beans and small carrots from the market a couple doors down. They looked delicious and were relatively inexpensive. Then I stopped into another little place and found fresh kiwi and raspberry sorbets that looked great. Not cheap but fun for all of us. I picked up a baguette from the artisanal *boulangerie* on the corner. Now I needed meat, and it was getting late.

The nearest butcher shop was absolutely crammed full with locals and I figured it would be easier to avoid it and just follow my nose, which almost immediately hit on the scent of rotisserie chicken coming from the (uncrowded and clearly high-end) shop just across the street. I quickly did the math and decided to go for it. The chicken would save time, and I had wasted quite a bit of it in the various shops I'd perused. I also thought it would save a bit of money since the lamb and pork I had seen at the butchers shops were definitely not cheap. Rotisserie was a win-win.

I walked in and was greeted by two smiling butchers. I said the few French words that I knew would get me what I wanted: *Poulet, si vous plait.* The first butcher made hand gestures that I interpreted to ask whether I wanted a "big chicken or small chicken." I gestured back, "I want a big chicken." The second butcher went to retrieve the bird. I chose a reasonable bottle of red table wine before getting in line to pay.

During my five or ten minutes in the shop, it went from relatively empty to packed house. The line was long with impatient French nobles behind me. When I reached the counter, the butcher said a few words—which I interpreted to be "great pick, your family will love you for this"—and then he rung me up (both literally and figuratively).

The bill came to €26, or around $38.00, *before* the wine. That's one expensive chicken.

But given the long line and butcher's work getting the thing off the spit and packaging it up, coupled with my total inability to communicate my discomfort with purchasing a near $40 chicken, I swallowed my pride and paid up with a smile.

Let's just say that I felt a bit "misled" as I walked home. But as I walked, I grew more and more confident. And by the time I walked through the door, the following words went through my mind, verbatim: "This is going to be a magical French chicken. Maybe the single best chicken the family has ever had."

The only thing magical about the chicken was its complete lack of flavor and juices. I had been given a chicken that had been rotisseried to death, probably a full day ago. Even Lily lamented that she had to take a sip of water with every bite. Wendi choked down a few nibbles. Kate refused it completely. I ate as much of it as I could muster, and the rest was tossed.

Here's another French word I know: *Merde*.

I spent the night tortured: Had I been blatantly screwed? Was there a miscommunication? Had I inadvertently asked for what I got? Misread a hand signal? What happened? How could I fall victim to the old "rotisserie chicken" scam?

I suppose it wasn't the (obscene) price so much but the fact that I had no idea what happened. If I couldn't understand a chicken deal in France, how could I possibly be trusted to understand one in Nepal or Turkey (no pun intended)? Sleep did not come easily.

I woke up the next morning and had to go get a SIM card but was feeling a bit gun-shy. I went anyway, sulking, and not only succeeded in finding a good deal on the card but also came across a French rail office we didn't know existed and was able to purchase discounted tickets for our impending train ride to Dijon. I returned home and triumphantly displayed fruits of my labor to my wife and children, who were clearly thrilled (at least that's how I saw it).

I've spent the past eight years getting married, raising kids and working long hours at an often difficult job, and I've forgotten a few things about living life on foreign soil. But the rotisserie chicken incident reminded me of something important.

You can take nothing for granted when you're on the road. Sometimes you win, and sometimes you take it on the, ah, chicken. Making a simple train connection can be daunting. Finding a meal that the kids will actually eat may be impossible. Running even the simplest errand can take hours.

Even purchasing a rotisserie chicken can be a nightmare.

It's challenging and exhilarating and tiring and fun and sometimes blows your mind. I love it, and I hope our family travels instill a similar sense of curiosity and wonder in Lily and Kate.

But I also hope that as they explore and find new people and places neither of them ever gets stuck with a $40 leather chicken.

C'est la vie!

CHAPTER 8
FROM PARIS WITH LOVE

Somewhere outside Dijon, France
July 2011

In Paris they simply stared when I spoke to them in French;
I never did succeed in making those idiots
understand their own language.
—Mark Twain

PARIS. The City of Light. Arguably the most romantic city on the planet. But forget all that, we were there with two kids! We didn't spend hours gazing into each other's eyeballs over candlelit dinners punctuated by aphrodisiacs and fine wines, and we did not spend day after day strolling the banks of the *Seine* with arms crossed or one hand in each other's back pocket. It just didn't happen. But we did have a great time and discover a different Paris, one that tolerated our (thankfully few) butchered attempts at the language and welcomed our kids and kept them (and us) happy and entertained.

First of all, we happened to be there for *Bastille Day*—effectively modern France's Fourth of July—and it was quite a show. I can confidently say that the French military puts on a mean parade. The real deal. From the *Arc de Triumph* up the

Champs Elysees to the *Obelisque* at the *Place de la Concorde*, and then over the *Seine* to the *National Assembly Building*, squadron after squadron of French soldiers, some proudly singing songs undoubtedly of French nationalism and others fiercely silent, marched in strict formation while decked out in full regalia (think swords and feathered caps).

There were gymnasts and firefighters doing carefully choreographed routines with ladders and trampoline people twisting and delighting and jets and paratroopers and helicopters. Row after row of heavy artillery and war machines were shined up and on display at *L'Hotel des Invalides*, with soldiers everywhere mingling with an enthusiastic public and explaining their implements of destruction.

This went on all day (really) and was followed up with a full pop concert and brilliant fireworks display on the *Champ du Mars* with the *Tour Eiffel* looming large and dominating the whole scene. It was pretty amazing and we soaked it all up, finally getting our awestruck children home for bed at midnight. Phew.

We spent hours in the *Jardin du Luxembourg*, playing on the massive playground, sailing toy boats in the shadow of *Luxembourg Palace* and appreciating the sculptures and flowers and general (jaw-dropping) beauty of the place. We saw a marionette show at the *Theatre du Luxembourg*, which the kids loved even though I am pretty sure they had little plot understanding since we were the sole Americans in attendance and the whole thing was in French. *Magnifique!*

We roamed the *Jardin des Tuileries*, rode the gigantic ferris wheel (with amazing views) and had some fun on the county fair-esque rides off of *Rue de Rivoli*. We climbed the *Eiffel Tower* (after *Bastille Day*), explored the *Musee d'Orsay* and admired *Notre Dame*. We ate a few terrific meals out—Lily learned that she likes *rillettes* and loves *pain au chocolate*—and a few good ones in the apartment (*The Rotisserie Chicken Incident* was one huge exception, of course). We snacked frequently on pastries and cookies and baguettes and meats and cheeses. We drank wine.

To me, though, the best times were not spent ogling particular sites or devouring meals or watching shows. Instead, I loved just *being in Paris* together. Watching Lily and Kate skipping past a cigarette-puffing shop owner on a quaint street, singing, then stopping to drool over window displays of macaroons or meringues. Exploring the narrow streets of the 5th Arrondissement or cruising *Rue de Dragon* or *Rue de Mouffetard* or *Rue de Lille* (a favorite, for obvious reasons, and just a block from our apartment).

Paris is just plain chock full of beauty and you see it everywhere, from the parks to the museums to the streets to the small shops. No amount of photographs (certainly those taken by us) can capture it.

Paris is an experience, a feeling. And we all got a taste of it. Wendi and I *did* have a few moments hand-in-hand on the *Seine* or sitting on a park bench or lazily strolling some unknown side street, with the girls laughing and playing 50 yards (ok, 25 yards) away. Lily and Kate *did* stop and ogle one beautiful thing or another, clearly recognizing that we were in a unique and different place.

But with that said, I actually think that the next time I'm in Paris, I will consciously spend less time rushing around to see everything and more time just *being in Paris*. In many ways, the girls forced us to do just that, and I am glad for it.

We left Paris by train this past Monday, heading south for Dijon and a barge/houseboat thingy on the *Rives de Saone* and canals in Burgundy and beyond. I was excited for this next leg of the journey but found it a bit difficult to leave too. I could hang out for awhile and get to know Paris a bit more. Learn some French, take a few cooking classes...you get the idea. But our plans and aspirations take us farther down a long road, and now is not the time for stopping. Not yet, anyway, and not here.

Farewell Paris, for now. We will meet again.

Je te verrais dans mes reves!

CHAPTER 9
A DEAR FRIEND

Still somewhere outside Dijon, France
July 2011

We call that person who has lost his father, an orphan;
and a widower that man who has lost his wife.
But that man who has known the immense unhappiness
of losing a friend, by what name do we call him?
Here every language is silent
and holds its peace in impotence.
—Joseph Roux,
French priest and philosopher

WENDI AND I LIVED on Maui for a few months right after we finished school at UCSB. We were sitting on a beach near our place in Kihei one afternoon when our conversation turned to the future and I distinctly remember what was said between us.

It was one of those pivotal moments in life; I knew it even then. And I think she did too.

Wendi suggested that we could stay on the islands, maybe. She could get her teaching credential and I could continue at the Four Seasons as a waiter and work my way up so we could spend our summers at fancy resorts in far off places.

I told her that was a potentially dangerous idea—because we *could* really do it. Might not be a bad life.

But I had (sort of) been thinking of law school and we ultimately decided to head back to the mainland to pursue a more conventional route. We planned that I would get a job in the legal business in an effort to figure out what lawyers actually do on a day-to-day basis before we jumped into a three year legal education and the mountain of debt that inevitably accompanies it.

I sent a (basically blank) resume to a number of law-related businesses around Santa Barbara. Paul Fritz, the owner of a small alternative dispute resolution firm called Creative Dispute Resolution (CDR), responded promptly with a telephone call and asked me a series of questions about my background and what I had been doing since graduation. It turned out that he loved Hawaii and surfing and guitars and he asked me to come in for an interview. He specifically requested that I bring my guitar along with me.

This was not exactly what the career people at UCSB told me to expect in a job search, but it was the beginning of a long and important relationship in my life.

The short story is that I got the job and ended up being at CDR for more than eighteen months. Paul was incredibly generous with his time and spent hours and hours talking with me about being a lawyer and answering my (probably ridiculous) questions. He indiscriminately introduced me to absolutely everybody he knew in town—judges, lawyers, secretaries, paralegals, business people. He took me with him to mediations and arbitrations as a "law student intern" and really showed me the nuts-and-bolts of the practice. It was an invaluable experience that I likely could not have duplicated anywhere else.

Paul encouraged me to "go to the best damn law school"

that would take me. And I did. I will never forget what he said to me after I had dinner with him and his wife at their home before I left Santa Barbara for school: "Congratulations, Matt. I will watch your career with great interest." Then he gave me a hug and I was off.

Paul was true to his word—this was a theme over the course of our friendship—and we kept in fairly close contact during the three years of school. I'd call with questions or to see how CDR was doing or to chat. He'd call to see how I was doing and offer his support and encouragement.

Paul drove to Berkeley to see my law school graduation and attend the relatively small party we threw. I remember that he was proud that I had finished at Boalt and was to litigate with a prominent San Francisco firm.

We kept in touch during the ensuing years too, much as we had before. I'd tell him how hard I was working and that it was going well. He'd tell me his old war stories and to keep at it, but he always stressed balance and prioritizing personal life and career, too. (These became important themes in my life.)

Paul and his wife came to my wedding in the Napa Valley. Our conversations and friendship grew deeper and in many ways more meaningful. He started offering (typically unsolicited) marital advice (always carefully considered and often right on the money). And when Wendi and I had Lily, he was chock full of advice and anecdotes. (He even provided written thoughts on a few occasions.) It became crystal clear to me that parenting and marriage were very important to Paul and he wanted to impart his experiences and related wisdom. I always listened and often discussed with Wendi.

I remember that Paul seemed excited when Wendi and the girls and I returned to Santa Barbara a few years back. And I know that he was excited when I decided to hang my own shingle, which was something he had counseled me to consider many times. He'd stop by my office or we'd meet at Harry's for a drink ("just one" he'd say, and then we'd end up sharing a second). He'd write me reminder notes on cocktail napkins, telling me to "D-E-L-E-G-A-T-E" more tasks or check out this book or talk to this tax guy or whatever. We talked about everything from owning a law office to practicing law to politics to history to parenting and marriage to cars to his beloved shotgun shooting (he'd taken me to the range a few times years ago) and who knows what else.

We were friends—had been for twelve years. We talked about life and aspirations and dreams and failures and successes. He was a trusted confidant and sounding board and I always valued his opinions and perspective.

It was difficult for me to tell Paul that I was closing my office to take time with my family and travel. In fact, he may have been the most difficult person for me to tell; I thought he'd be disappointed that I was taking some time off from a new office that was doing well.

But when I finally met him at Harry's for a drink a week before we left, it turned out that I was wrong. He was thrilled for Wendi and me and the kids, and repeatedly congratulated us. You see, Paul had litigated and owned a law practice. Paul was married and had kids. Paul had taken time and traveled with his family.

And Paul understood me much better than I imagined.

I lost track of time as we talked about the impending trip and everything else, and I had to run out of Harry's pretty quickly to meet Wendi and the girls at a dinner. Before I left, we exchanged our typical embrace and I gave him a kiss on the cheek and I looked him in the eye and I thanked him. He just smiled, proudly, and told me to have fun with my wife and kids.

Paul died on July 10, 2011, suddenly. After we left for

Europe, he developed a cough, which became so bad that he was eventually unable to speak. When he went to see the doctor, he learned that he had gone through a series of small strokes and, ultimately, that he had advanced pancreatic cancer. He died, amongst family, within a couple weeks. My deepest and most sincere thoughts are with his wife and children.

Paul was more than a longtime friend to me, he was an important mentor and father figure in many ways and I am shocked and terribly saddened by his passing. He taught me many things: to be courteous yet direct, to stand up for what I believe in, the value of preparedness, the need to take time for reflection and family. He was a good man, and I am better for knowing for him. I will miss his surprise visits to the office, breakfasts at the Cajun Kitchen, his good advice over a Bushmills at Harry's, his handwritten notes (many of which remain in the "Paul Fritz" file in my now shuttered office). I will miss our conversations and his sometimes quirky perspective that I valued so much.

I guess I will miss most everything about him. And I won't forget our many good times together or his smile at Harry's just a month ago.

—•—

It has taken me over a week to write this, and in that time I tried to think about what Paul's death means as it relates to the traveling I am doing with my wife and daughters. (This is supposed to be about traveling with my family, after all.) I'd love to say that his death is a clear demonstration of the need to really live your life for today and do the things you want to do. One could certainly see it that way, however bittersweet. And I think Paul would see some truth and wisdom in that way of thinking. I certainly do.

But there is a flip side of that coin, too. I can't shake the feeling that I would have loved to see him one last time, and to tell him how important he has been in my life. I think he knew (just as I knew how proud he was of me), but I still would've liked to tell him. So maybe his death is a reminder of the importance of staying close to the ones you love. I think Paul would have seen wisdom and truth in that too. I certainly do.

Maybe this was Paul's point all along. Balance is the key. Do the things that make you happy, but recognize that there are competing (important) concerns and do your best to temper one with the other. Sounds simple enough, but it is not always easy and you can't have it both ways.

Wendi and I always said that we could take our trip and come back to Santa Barbara and everything would be just as we left it. While that may be true in many respects, it is decidedly false in at least one very important way. I nevertheless continue to believe that we made the right choice for us; taking a break and spending this time together as a family has been incredible already. But it would be disingenuous to suggest that our decision is without drawbacks.

Paul's death is a harsh lesson in that regard.

CHAPTER 10
MY MISTRESS, THE COUNTESS

Lyon, France
July 2011

---

*I've got a little, a little poem that I'd like to read
in honor of this occasion, if I may.
Spaulding get your foot off the boat!*
—Judge Smails

I LOVED HER THE MOMENT I laid eyes on her.

She sat idle in the radiant Burgundy sun, seductive, bored; French in every aspect of the word. Her lines and curves took my breath away, if only for a moment, and then she filled my chest with warmth and perfumes of the sort found only in the French countryside. She was dignified, a royal, but her seemingly impenetrable pedigree was softened and broken the moment my wildly excited kids piled on top of her, poking, prodding, pushing her buttons.

My French mistress was a thirty foot, seven ton, river-cruising barge called *Countess Thirteen*, and we'd leased her for a week. She was to be our home for a lazy self-guided tour of the *Saone River* and canals in and around Burgundy and beyond.

The "boat trip" was one of the first things we planned, many months ago, and expectations were pretty high. We figured that spending some time on a boat doing very little would be good for all of us after a full month of traveling. The whole idea was to have some good, clean family fun. We were armed with games and art supplies and my guitar, and had rented a few bikes to ride through the towns we'd explore during the week. It was a good and well-intentioned plan (mostly Wendi's idea), and represented much of what we want over the course of our travels.

We didn't really consider the inevitable moments mooring and otherwise parking the *Countess* that tested our marital fortitude. Or the highly stressed cursing and spitting that accompanied our early navigation of the first locks upriver. (For those of you who don't know, as we didn't, these "locks" are man-made devices that raise or lower your boat as you head up or down river, respectively. On the *Saone*, they are ancient, narrow and unforgiving places. Thus the cursing. And the spitting.)

That reminds me. There is a classic moment seared into my memory in which I was doing my best, I swear, to drive that damn boat out of a tight spot in the harbor at *Auxonne* under breezy conditions. I succeeded in turning the whole boat—a monstrous and not exactly nimble French rental—the wrong way and accidentally sliding stern-first into a thankfully empty private slip between two rather large and expensive boats. Things seemed to be going from bad to worse as the winds picked up and tension rose and Wendi began scrambling around the bow to push us free of the yachts around us while telling me—in ever-escalating terms—to, um, do a better job of driving (always a healthy conversation piece). But then a bent old Englishman magically appeared from the cabin of the bigger and more ostentatious of the two endangered boats and yelled, with a chuckle, "They're bloody pigs in wind, aren't they?" We laughed and drove away, tension diffused and marital balance restored.

Where was I? Oh, cursing and spitting and tension aside, the whole *Countess* crew eventually calmed down and worked together as one, rendering any purported obstacle (relatively) easily overcome. Wendi used sheer strength and power to haul lines under difficult conditions; Lily barked commands to "make the boat turn, daddy" while Kate's watchful eye looked for anything out of the ordinary. *Countess* was in capable hands.

Lily and Kate eventually took turns driving the boat, and we soon realized that they—with an aggregate age of 9—could effectively handle steering the barge without major issue. Wendi and I played Gin Rummy and Solitaire and Uno and War and Trouble with each other and the kids while listening to a bizarre yet fantastic classic French/1980s American music station. (To give you a sense, we sang along with "Total Eclipse of the Heart" three times and had our fill of disco hits and Madonna and Michael Jackson interspersed with tons of French/Parisian classics.) We spent some timing sketching a swan—affectionately named "Blanc" and voted a temporary family pet in Bucky the dog's absence—that followed us for awhile. (There were dozens of swan on the river and every time she saw one, Kate screamed "Blanc!," apparently shocked that he kept finding us.) I played a reasonable amount of guitar.

We rode bikes in the countryside along the *Saone* and explored a few rural French towns. It rained a couple times, and once we were caught in a downpour on the bikes far from the boat. We lucked into a little restaurant where the staff understood no English and we successfully conveyed absolutely nothing in French. Wendi and I ended up with a fondue to share and a great bottle of wine, and the kids ate chicken and French fries. We waited the storm out watching

Le Tour projected onto a high wall and playing foosball and pool in the bar.

Maybe the best thing of all, though, was that we had to work together as a family to make the week enjoyable and fun; I think we did a good job in that regard. When I needed some time to myself, I went for a run on the banks of the river, sometimes with Lily riding a bike alongside. (On one such occasion, I taught her how to shift gears on a small mountain bike and she was thrilled with her newfound hill-climbing prowess and downhill speeds.) Wendi would head into town on a bike by herself or go for a morning jog.

We talked for hours.

I learned a lot about my own kids, frankly, many things I didn't know before. Turns out that they are sentient, thinking little beings. And they're pretty damned cool to hang out with.

Wendi and I spent the nights sipping wine or eating chocolate cookies and whispering to each other (for fear of waking the girls) over a game of cards we both secretly wanted to win. That kind of time together, in that setting (nobody around, nothing to do, stunningly beautiful vistas, etc.), will be hard to duplicate on this trip or any other. I already have fond memories.

This was just the type of experience that we wanted when we made our plans, and we got it aboard the *Countess*. We spent hours and hours together and had a blast. Yes, there were difficult times with crying kids or less-than-perfect boatmanship, but we ultimately tamed the river and spent a relaxing week floating around the French countryside. What else can I say?

(Other than, perhaps, that I have no need for a mistress, French or otherwise. My wife is just fine.)

We got off the boat a week ago and had no plan—seriously—

other than to head to Lyon to pick up our long-term rental car (a Renault Twingo; what, you've never heard of a Twingo?). We were still hunting for accommodations in the late afternoon and, finally, after a few hours of haphazard internet searches and guidebook guesswork, we successfully rented an apartment we'd never seen in a town in which we'd never been in a neighborhood we knew nothing about.

We circled the general area in which the apartment was supposed to be for another hour, finally realizing that it was only accessible by foot and that very few people actually knew the address. The girls were starving and crying out for sustenance. Wendi and I were tired and, well, *irritable*. (Let's just say that my driving was again a conversation piece.)

So, *this* is traveling without any plans.

CHAPTER 11
THE END OF FRENCH ADVENTURE PARKS

Lyon, France
July 2011

You see, fear causes hesitation,
and hesitation will cause your worst fears to come true.
—Bodhi

WE'VE BEEN IN LYON for a few days and really love the city. It is a terrific place and we highly recommend it for anyone heading to France: great food, great sites, great people. In fact, it's maybe our favorite stop yet. More on that soon.

We were talking with a friendly French father yesterday and he told us about a nearby "adventure park" that we might enjoy. The truth is that we are really coming into our own as a traveling family at this point, and we are getting a good feeling for the sorts of days that are likely to be fun. And anything that happens to involve "adventure," for example, is reasonably likely to also involve happy children.

And that, of course, is good.

This particular "adventure" would take us up the side of a mountain in a "fun-icular" and past a wonderful cathedral that we had chosen as a site worth seeing. So we quickly decided to follow the kind Frenchman's advice and give the "adventure park" a try.

Lily was (shockingly) electrified when we figured out that we'd be spending our day strapped into mountain climbing harnesses overcoming dreadful obstacles high up in the canopy of a forest. She was young enough to need a "chaperone" and didn't actually meet the height requirements but nobody seemed to care (hey, we're talking centimeters here, not inches!), so I was on the hook. (Wendi and Kate sat this one out, opting instead for some mini-courses designed for kids and a picnic on the ground far below Lily and me.)

We spent a couple hours learning about carabiners and zip lines and honing our new skills on small-but-still-some-what-intimidating ropes courses. Lily was a quick study and followed the rules carefully. I was soon (over?) confident in her ability, even despite the fact that she giggled uncontrollably nearly the whole time.

We eventually decided to move up to the "big boy" course. But there was a line at the bottom of the relevant ladder that would have taken a half-hour and Lily was anxious to keep going. One of the eighteen-year olds who was "supervising" the operation suggested that we come back later and try the "biggest zip line" up the hill in the meantime. Lily was thrilled with the idea, so we headed up.

We marched quite a long way up the hill and soon found ourselves standing alone at the bottom of a rope ladder that seemed to go up into the clouds. (I'm talking Jack and the frickin' Beanstalk.) Lily looked up, giggled, and adeptly locked her carabiners into place and began climbing. I followed her up, suspicious of what might be in store.

After successfully meeting a few challenges high up in the treetops, we emerged onto a tiny platform that had barely enough room for both of us. We were a solid fifty feet up off the ground (ah, come on, that's only sixteen meters!), and there were literally hundreds of feet of zip line in front of us.

The French guy was right: This was undoubtedly the "biggest zip line." Maybe in the whole world.

My first thoughts were these:

This is too big. Way too big. We should head down the easy way.

And I was right. One hundred percent. I knew I was right then and I am positive I was right now. But this was sort of like hiking up to an out-of-bounds quadruple black diamond at the end of a long day while ski-patrol is looking for you. There was no turning back.

Lily strapped in, nonchalantly, and giggled. I checked her rig and she was perfectly positioned and ready to go. Then, as I stared, eyes gaping and chin brushing the ground far below, she waved and leapt off the platform into the abyss.

I knew it was bad from the moment she took off.

Her wonderful, tiny body shot off as though she had a jet-pack attached to her back. And it became clear all too soon that she wouldn't be slowing down as others before her had; she was actually *too small* for this particular line. Big people with death wishes—you know, *adrenaline seeking adults*—for whom this God-forsaken hellish nightmare was designed, would take off, much as my first born daughter had just done, and their weight would get them going. Their weight would then cause the enormously long zip line to dip toward the ground such that the entire second half of the ride would effectively be going up the zip line, thereby slowing the heavy adult down and causing him or her to drift up to the second platform reasonably slowly, leading to an easy dismount and a bunch of laughing and smiling.

But Lily had no weight. So the line didn't dip toward the

earth. So she never went up the zip line. So she never slowed down.

And so she sped across the void at an undeniably dangerous speed, smashed into the (mercifully) well-padded tree trunk hundreds of feet away from me and missed the platform.

She didn't dismount.

Instead, as I stood incredulous and stunned back on the initial platform from whence she came, Lily sped back on to the zip line, now heading *backward*, toward me, at a high rate of speed. I could barely make out the disconcerted cries spewing forth from her lips. I definitely heard Wendi, however, inexplicably sounding totally unconcerned from the field far below us (hey, who drank that cheap French table wine in our bag?), when she yelled: "Don't worry, honey, Daddy will come get you. He'll, well, *he'll come bump you!*"

I paused. Time actually stood still. I'm not trained for zip line rescue; I'm a lawyer for Christ's sake. How in the hell am I going to "bump her" to safety? Can this damned zip line even hold both of us?

A million thoughts raced through my mind as I watched Lily slow to a stop and dangle helplessly high above a beautiful but ominously unforgiving French field far below. Primarily, I recall thinking how indisputably bad my parenting had been for a number of reasons: (1) We were WAY TOO FAR OFF THE GROUND FOR IT TO BE COMPREHENSIBLE THAT MY SIX YEAR OLD DAUGHTER WOULD BE SAFE as she hurled her beautiful, wonderful, naïve self across that abysmal void; (2) the 250-FOOT ZIP LINE THAT REQUIRED SIGNIFICANT VELOCITY FOR SUCCESSFUL NAVIGATION BY EVEN GROWN MEN was obviously highly inappropriate for my kid; and (3) NEITHER LILY NOR I HAD ANY RELEVANT EXPERIENCE THAT MIGHT HAVE MADE THIS POTENTIALLY DISASTROUS ACT ANYTHING LESS THAN EXTRAORDINARILY DANGEROUS.

Setting that aside for now, though, please steady yourself and take a stab at what happened next:

a. Lily plunged to the ground, ending the day with substantial injury and parents in a French jail on endangerment and neglect charges.

b. Lily spent two full hours terrified and suspended from the ground by more than ten times her height (with a great view of Lyon!) while a rescue effort was planned and carried out. Wendi and I were arrested and tossed into a French jail on endangerment and neglect charges.

c. Lily burst into tears and vowed to neither forgive nor trust me ever again.

d. I hightailed my ass out on to that *&%$#!@ horrifying zip line without hesitation to save my kid's life, inwardly stressed to near cardiovascular failure and high on adrenaline but outwardly displaying the toothy, wide-eyed grin of a lunatic and laughing insanely in an effort to keep my young daughter calm under, shall we say, less than ideal circumstances.
(Drum roll.)

If you chose d., go buy yourself a Boilermaker or six, just as I did the moment we hit *terra firma*. The good news is that I was indeed able to "bump" my kid across that line (with substantial effort that I calmly dispensed while keeping Lily calm and laughing, I might add). And Lily thought the whole scene a riot and never blinked an eye. I think that there was little or no permanent damage, and we have seen no signs of PTSD to date.

I guess that just about does it for French adventure parks.

CHAPTER 12
AN INCONVENIENT TRUTH

San Lorenzo, Italy
August 2011

I did not have sexual relations with that woman.
—William Jefferson Clinton

S ORRY FOR BEING SO DISTANT, but there's a reason we haven't said much lately. I guess I'm not entirely sure how best to say this but at least one thing is clear: We simply cannot continue this charade any longer.

It would be unfair to both of us.

Look, we're not proud of what we've done. There's no doubt about that. And, well, I'm stalling.

The truth is that we've been *cheating* on you.

Wait! Please don't go! Before you jump up and run off, let us explain our inadvertent infidelity. We didn't mean to destroy the trust and confidence we've built together and we really want you to stay. We didn't mean for it to happen and we won't do it again. Ever. We promise.

You see, traveling around the world is supposed to be *hard*. And it has been, we swear. Running around new and unfamiliar places, moving every few days, planning the logistics of the whole operation, sightseeing... it's downright exhausting.

So exhausting, in fact, that when we got to Torino after driving across the French/Italian border from Lyon, we just couldn't do it anymore. We spent a lazy day and night strolling the covered sidewalks of Italy's first capital (and site of the 2006 Winter Olympics!), admiring grand *piazzas* and *palazzos* and gobbling pizzas and gelatos.

We didn't see the very famous *Shroud of Turin*. We didn't go to the "best Egyptian museum outside of Cairo." In fact, other than the few sites we were able to make out over our heaping helpings of glorious gelato that effectively eclipsed our collective field of vision, we didn't see (or do) much of anything.

We tried but we couldn't, we swear.

We were plain tuckered out.

So, late that night, after the kids were fast asleep (around midnight in light of the metric ton of sugar they'd consumed in the form of a particular Italian frozen treat), Wendi and I conspired. We colluded. We took out the computer and we searched. And we found. And we couldn't resist.

Maybe you should sit down for this.

Early the next morning, we quietly packed our things and left Torino in the *Twingo* a few days early. We spoke not a word of our destination to anyone. We could barely speak of it amongst ourselves.

Because we were cheating. And we knew it.

So, ok, here it is: We drove five hours—it was only one or two out of our way—to a little cabana we'd rented at a family-oriented beachside resort on the Tuscan coast. We spent the next five days playing in the Mediterranean on a private beach and parading around swimming pools with Italian families and all the truly wonderful things that come along with them. There were delightful fresh foods that all of us loved and frequently devoured. There was perfect weather.

There were sunset walks in the sand. (The sunsets were so slow and incredible that Kate asked, with big tired eyes as she and I were walking back from the beach to our bungalow in the forest together on one of the warm nights, deadly serious, "Does the sun sleep in the sea, Daddy?")

There were poolside exercise classes and saunas and go-carts and happy Italian families pinching our children's cheeks and yelling "*Bellissima!*" and there were speedos and water aerobics and techno-music (with sometimes wildly inappropriate yet nearly universally misinterpreted or misunderstood English lyrics) and new friends and beach toys and cocktails and water slides and boogie boards and a quaint Italian seaside village and and and...

And I've said too much.

We are supposed to regale you with tales of vomiting kids and forgotten passports and the hassles of purchasing rotisserie chickens in Parisian markets. But there are no such stories this time. (Indeed, the worst it got was a series of short arguments between Wendi and me over who was entitled to the third cup of shockingly delightful, jet black, oily-yet-silky-smooth and heavily narcotic Italian coffee in the mornings.) There're only a few glorious days of bliss under the Tuscan sun in the gentle waters of the Mediterranean. It was a taste of home for us in many ways and we had a truly fantastic time.

And we are sorry.

Despite the fact that we didn't see a damned site—not a single one!—we got a much-deserved vacation from our vacation and experienced a real Italian family-style holiday. We were the only Americans in a resort that was sort of 1950s *Dirty Dancing* meets a more modern beach vacation. We met lots of real Italian families and our kids met lots of real Italian kids. We talked parenting and marriage and business and politics and economics and got an often educated and thoughtful perspective on American-ism and Italian-ism. It was a fantastic experience that we didn't mean to have, but it worked out and it happened and we loved it.

And we will never do it again.

You have our word.

— · —

We left *Riva degli Etruschi* on Thursday, and headed inland to *Barbialla Nuova*, the first organic farm we'll be working on in exchange for room and board. None of us have any farming experience, organic or otherwise, but we have wanted to learn more about it for a long time and thus signed up for "WWOOF Italia" (WWOOF stands for World-Wide Opportunities on Organic Farms, and there are WWOOF organizations in many countries around the world that are focused on teaching and sharing sustainable farming and living). That's how we found *Barbialla*, a working cattle ranch in the middle of Tuscany that is willing to help us get our hands dirty. We will be here for two weeks before heading to a second farm further south in Tuscany for another two.

So, notwithstanding our highly inappropriate beachside roll-in-the-hay with the Italian families for which we are deeply sorry and regret-filled, I'm sure there'll be more than enough ill-fated farm work and child labor-related catastrophes over the next month to win you back.

Trust us.

CHAPTER 13
FARM AID

Montaione, Italy
August 2011

---

*Family farmers are innovative entrepreneurs who
safeguard our food, environment and health.*
—Willie Nelson

"I HOPE YOU AREN'T ONE of these Tea Party supporters."
Those were the first words we heard from Ken, one of
our WWOOF hosts at *Barbialla Nuova*, a 1200-acre organic farm
in Tuscany. He was finishing lunch with his wife, Amy, and
their two kids (aged 6 and 3, just like ours!), when we walked
through the front door of their farmhouse. Ken happened to be
finishing an article about Michele Bachmann, and was basically
horrified that she could be seriously considered by anyone for
President of the United States given the colorful sorts of things
she was saying about a variety of social issues, as well as her
positions on solving America's debt problem and taxation.

I quickly read the article and was, frankly, a bit embarrassed.

We spent the next hour sitting around Ken and Amy's
kitchen table talking about the American political landscape and
process and various politicians and economics and social issues
and people's perceptions of all of the foregoing. This is not a

political commentary—and I won't reveal too much about my own personal views—but I must say that the recent debt ceiling "debate" and the "solutions" to the debt problem being tossed around Washington (not to mention the simmering health care "debate"), coupled with the views being expressed by some of our newer (designer) "politicians" seem increasingly ridiculous. Admittedly, I don't have the same day-to-day insight that I had while sitting behind my desk for hours at a time and checking various media outlets, but I can confidently say that something is broken. And the world is watching as the Bachmanns and Palins (and others, both male and female) of Washington run amuck and say whatever comes to mind on *Twitter* or some reality show or from some other modern soapbox.

Let's just say that they are not exactly instilling confidence that our politicians will be able to effectively govern a country that some would argue was once a model for political, religious, social and economic freedoms. And their (sometimes loud, seemingly uneducated and/or blatantly offensive) words and actions are viewed as reflections of the values held by me and you and our kids.

I am a proud American and truly believe that we live in one of the great societies on the planet. And I am all for diversity of political and economic and social views. But think before you vote, my friends. Think before you vote.

So. Life on the farm. It's good, man.

After we finished sitting around and chatting like old friends, Amy took us up the dirt road, past the beef cows and field of wildflowers to our rustic little apartment. We moved in and got comfortable, and then helped set up for a weekly dinner put on for the guests of the ranch—*Barbialla* is an *agriturismo* and has a few villas scattered around that can house an aggregate 30 or 40 people for weekly stays on the property. The authentic Tuscan meal was delicious, and so was the locally produced organic wine. We met guests from all over Europe and sat and ate and drank and talked with them. It was a perfect introduction to the farm and we really enjoyed it, staying up late with Ken and Amy and their kids to finish the clean up.

On Friday, I woke early and spent the day with Ken learning all about and baking bread, starting with nothing more than flour, water and salt at first light. Ken is a self-described "bread-head" and has a real passion and talent for all things bread-related. After spending many years working and baking on his family's farm in his native southern Australia (Amy is an Aussie as well, from Adelaide), he spent some time traveling the world and ultimately studied the art and science of bread baking in, of all places, Massachusetts. (He also spent a few months in Sonoma County, just outside of Healdsburg, and very near my hometown.) Since then, Ken has worked in a variety of small and large bakeries around the world and seriously knows his stuff. (Seriously.) He's a real artisan bread-maker.

I learned a ton and had a great time participating in the process from helping light the wood-fired bread oven Ken built to brushing the finished loaves—which are sold in the small farm store and to a few local restaurants and families—as they came out of it many hours later. I worked with and shaped dough and learned some of the intricacies of the trade from a guy who makes it all look very easy. (It's not.) We finished the day with some truly delicious pizzas in the oven for all to share. Think prosciutto, mushrooms and fresh herbs, tomato and basil, and other mouthwatering combinations from Ken's mind and the organic garden out back. You'd never have imagined that we'd get through six pizzas but they went quickly, washed down with cold Belgian beer.

We spent the weekend mostly relaxing around and otherwise enjoying the farm. It is warm but not "unbearably hot" as many warned of Italy in August, and we had meals with Ken and Amy and the family and got to know a few of the other people working on the farm. We took the Twingo to the walled city of Volterra on Sunday and had a great time exploring its narrow streets and Roman, Etruscan and medieval ruins.

Tuscany is gorgeous.

Monday morning brought our first full work day as WWOOFers, and we were not totally sure what to expect. We walked to work as a family (fun!) and received our assignment: Learn how to build a "hot compost" and then do it, and work around the organic garden pruning and weeding and ultimately picking the fruits and vegetables that are ready to be sold in the farm store that caters to guests and interested passersby.

We all got started together, Wendi doing one thing or another with one kid and me doing something else with the other, switching jobs so that everybody got a chance to do everything, really enjoying our work. Both Ken and Amy are super involved and knowledgeable about sustainable farming and smaller-scale garden work (amongst other things) so we effectively got a personalized class in that regard. The kids eventually broke away and Wendi and I got to work with Ken and Amy (and Ken's recently-arrived friend Jeff, another friendly Aussie with lots of green farming experience) gathering hay and green material and shoveling cow and chicken poop for the compost bin. (I can now proudly check "cow poop slurry making" off of my list of things to do.) Then we built the hot compost, which is basically a layer cake of hay, green material and poop slurry (the chicken feces "really sets it off," according to Amy). We finished the day with a lovely little Risotto with fresh green beans from the farm and locally raised chicken and some local red wine. Wow.

The next day, we spent a few hours picking blackberries for the organic jam we'd eventually make for the farm store.

(Wendi and the girls had already started this process while I was baking with Ken, so we had a good start.) We wandered the property together, picking (and eating) blackberries under the warm morning sun. We found loads—as the Aussies might say—of berries and got back just in time for another wonderful lunch. Then a short siesta followed by jam-making well into the evening. We shared a catered dinner with Ken and Amy and the farm's owner that was put together by a local Tuscan woman who was auditioning for a job. Delightful, again, and another late night, playing guitar, sipping Chiantis or other local wines, enjoying each other's company in a beautiful setting without many other people around.

I've been writing this for a few days now but things keep happening that feel worthy so I keep waiting to finish it up. At this point, though, it's clear that there may never be a perfect moment. I guess all I can say is that we have also harvested lavender, pruned and tended to a small group of wine grapes, trimmed rose bushes, bottled wine and labeled jam jars. And we've done it all together, as a family, under the instruction of another family that takes pride in and is very knowledgeable and willing to teach us about sustainable, organic farming and cooking and living.

And we are not paying a dime to be here. Our room and board is covered by the work we are doing.

That is the true beauty of WWOOFing, and we are believers. So much so, in fact, that we are talking to Amy and Ken about other WWOOFing connections in New Zealand and Australia. (Amy and Ken and their kids spent a year going around the world WWOOFing and doing many of the same types of things we are doing; in fact, that is how they found *Barbialla*, and they will have been here for 18 months before returning to mother Australia.)

On a personal level, I find the work we've done really

satisfying and am confident that we can and will take some of it home and put it to use. All of us are learning a lot here on the farm, and the kids are enjoying the garden work and other tasks (not to mention the cows and chickens, especially the "Bad Chicken," but that is for another time). Sometimes I am reminded very much of growing up in Sonoma County, spending the summers running around in the woods in the heat without too much real danger or trouble. This kind of time with the kids and each other is really rewarding and I am grateful that we discovered WWOOFing and *Barbialla* and especially Ken and Amy and their brood.

Tonight after Wendi finished her turn baking with Ken and we devoured more delicious pizzas and beer, we all helped put together a beautiful lasagna with fresh eggplant and zucchini from the garden. Amy nonchalantly threw together a fresh blackberry/apple crumble from scratch. We put everything in the still-hot bread oven (including some additional roasted veggies) and walked up to a private pond for sunset. Nobody around, a small pier to dive or jump off, warm and clean and refreshing water, a brilliant sunset and fast-rising full moon, kids laughing and jumping into the water, then picking wildflowers and blackberries from the high branches off of our shoulders. We brought some wine and sipped it from the bottle as we walked back to find a perfectly cooked meal waiting for us. It was maybe the best lasagna I've ever had—really—and some reheated pizza and left over pasta salad and Amy's crumble left all of us full and groggy. The kids went to bed smiling.

So did we.

Life on the farm, man…it's good.

———•———

We are taking this weekend off and heading to Venice by train for a couple days. We had talked about doing Venice after the WWOOFing experiences (we are headed to a second farm soon) but we are rapidly approaching the end of all the formal plans we made and things are already beginning to move a bit as those around us make good suggestions. We are now actively talking about next steps and expect to begin planning phase two a bit more earnestly (very) soon.

Right now, I suppose that there is only one thing we can say with absolute certainty: We ain't ready for home yet.

So stay tuned.

CHAPTER 14
DESPERATE MEASURES

Venice, Italy
August 2012

Better safe than sorry.
—English Proverb

WE LOST KATE in Venice.

Back to that in a sec.

We'd heard and read so many good things about Venice that our imaginations ran wild and expectations were perhaps higher than anywhere else we'd been.

And in this fairly rare circumstance, not only were those expectations met but they were exceeded.

Venice is *cool*. Despite the widely known and generally accepted fact that it is literally overrun by tourists (it is), it still feels authentic and relevant and old worldly and...*cool*. So cool, in fact, that we were in what could fairly be described as a water bus accident on the *Canal Grande* within twenty minutes of our arrival and nobody even batted an eye.

Octogenarians were violently thrown to the floor and children were knocked sideways and over and down amongst a sea of toppled and tussled tourists in a near frenzied state of panic. I gathered the girls close, immediately fearing a mutiny that may have resulted in our indefinite detention aboard a Venetian *Vaporetto*.

But, alas, there was no mutiny. The locals just got up, dusted themselves off and went on their way. The bus driver (captain?) didn't apologize or otherwise acknowledge a clear mistake: I think he accidently hit "full forward" rather than "reverse," causing the boat to lurch recklessly forward and eventually ram the floating bus stop at no fewer than 15 knots (that's a rough speed estimate given that my "miles per hour to knots" conversion equation may be best described as loosely based on what I believe may be accurate).

There was no checking to be sure that nobody was injured. There wasn't even any checking of the boat to be sure it remained sea worthy. There was just a quick stop, then a herd of crazed people stampeding toward the relative safety of the sidewalk followed by the driver taking off at breakneck speed again, nearly ripping the cleat from the dock due to the inadequate time he allowed his crew to deal with the lines. And then, suddenly, the angry and frightened masses on the sidewalk mellowed, mesmerized by the wonder and spectacle that is Venice. Smiles appeared. Cameras clicked. Cocktails were ordered.

Balance was restored.

We got into our apartment and spent the evening (and some of the night) casually strolling the ancient narrow streets and alleys and generally soaking up all things Venice. We stopped and gazed from the *Rialto Bridge*—which itself seemed to glow in the gentle sunset light—down the *Canal Grande* and saw countless Gondolas and water taxis and fat boats and skinny boats and long boats and short boats all dancing together on the waterways, creating a general havoc and nearly crashing but with drivers laughing and yelling and putting on a wonderful show that appealed to all people without bias. We pondered the bright lights that dimmed magically in their reflection off of the still waters of neighborhood canals and listened to Gondoliers sing and whistle and watched lovers kiss as they glided silently under flowered bridges, champagne in hand, nearly spilling. We bought masks and laughed and joked. We stood in awe of *Piazza San Marco*.

We fell in love with Venice, and with each other. We went to bed late, tired and happy.

And we did the same thing the next day.

And the next.

Venice is quite possibly the most unique place I've been. There were times—and I don't mean to devalue or demean the experience in any way—when I literally thought that I was in Disneyland. But then I'd look around and remind myself that this is a real city that has been around for over a thousand years. People *live* in Venice. Its legendary beauty, opulence, creativity, arts, parties, power...it's all infectious and intoxicating. It grows on you and it changes you, even if only for the time that you are there and surrounded by it. It slows you down. It calms you down. It soothes.

Put it on the list, if you haven't already.

It's worth it.

Ok, so, back to Kate. We lost her.

It was only for a moment, even less than a minute, but it was terrifying. We'd lost her once before, in Paris, just outside the *Musee d'Orsay*. But she was collected quickly by a museum employee and returned before you could say "Holy %$#@, we've lost our child!" We vowed then never to let either kid out of our site for the rest of the trip. And we succeeded in that regard, until this past Sunday morning.

Here is what I know: We were all drooling and smacking

our lips over a smorgasbord of beautiful pastries at a little café next to the *Canal Grande*. Wendi and I ordered, and we looked to Lily to see if she had made a decision. She ordered a chocolate croissant (we are still not quite past France on that one). We looked to Kate. But Kate was gone.

For those of you who have never lost a child, there is a rapid escalation of terror and panic that feeds on itself. Think of the Homeland Security Advisory System (also known as the "Terror Alert System"), which starts with the benign green-colored "Low" rating, then rises, in ever more frightening colors and language from "Guarded" to "Elevated" to "High" to "Severe," which is bright red and warns of a "SEVERE RISK OF TERRORIST ATTACKS." I suppose that parents could create a Lost Child Panic Rating Matrix, which would go something like this:

1. **Low**. This is the simple realization that your kid isn't around. There is no real fear or panic at this level. ("Our child is not in our immediate view but s/he is around, s/he always is.")

2. **Guarded**. The good parent in you (finally) suggests that you should find your kid, so you begin looking. This is often accompanied by a twinge of embarrassment. ("Our child has wandered off due to our momentary neglect and we need to find him/her before we [insert family activity].")

3. **Elevated**. A hint of frustration and anger creeps in here as you can't find your kid and s/he won't respond after a few meaningful attempts to retrieve him/her. People start looking at you and rolling their eyes. ("We think our misbehaved child is probably hiding from us (again) and s/he won't respond or show him/herself.") But anger quickly gives way to discomfort.

4. **High**. Parents begin to look at each other for answers and

start to move more quickly and call more earnestly. The realization-that-your-kid-may-really-be-missing camel starts to poke its nose under the tent and discomfort quickly gives way to full-fledged fear. This is tremendously unsettling and builds rapidly, feeding on itself and playing tricks on your mind. Parents look at each other helplessly and non-verbal communication takes over. (This is the "Holy %$#@, we've lost our child!" moment that Wendi and I narrowly avoided in Paris. It is also the threshold of hell.)

5. **Severe**. Panic. Hysteria. Sheer terror. Running, screaming, arms waiving, wild-eyed lunacy. It's instinctual, triggered by something deep down inside of each and every parent that exists for only this moment. It's serious and it's terrifying and I never want either my wife or myself to have to endure it again. ("My kid is gone and I will do anything it takes to get him/her back, right now, and I don't care about anything else. This is not a joke.")

Wendi and I spent just a few seconds at Level Five, but it felt an eternity. The associated panic is contagious, you see, and people around you stop rolling their eyes and start listening to you and doing whatever they can to help. We'd been screaming and running and searching and losing it for only a few horrifying seconds—now thinking of Venice's twisting labyrinth of streets and alleys and canals and waterways as something far more sinister—when some Dutch youngsters asked whether our Kate had blond hair. "YES!" we screamed in unison and they pointed down the street, right to where Kate was sitting patiently waiting for her breakfast.

She wanted to find us a table on the big canal, she said.

Then she burst into tears.

We all took a deep breath and had breakfast. We spent the morning much as we had the other days, but by lunch we were exhausted. We found a small table at a small restaurant in a small courtyard on the water, without too many people around, sat down and had a lovely (and significantly over-budget) bottle of fizzy pink wine and an *aperitivo* or two. We watched Lily and Kate laugh and sing and dance and play together against a stunning Venice backdrop. We relaxed.

After the wine bottle was turned upside-down in the bucket, Wendi and I talked of how lucky we were that morning. And we seriously discussed something that we had always joked about before.

We talked about buying a leash for our kid. You know, one of those ridiculous contraptions that has the look of a cheap backpack and the utility of a dog harness or an umbilical cord or a fricking lasso from the old west? Let's just say it was on the table.

You know what they say about desperate times.

We finished the day grateful, with a romantic Gondola ride at sunset, and left the next morning heading back to the farm where there are acres and acres for Kate to explore under our (very) watchful eyes.

CHAPTER 15
ANSWERING AN AGE-OLD QUESTION

Monteriggioni, Italy
August 2011

When the man who feeds the world by toiling in the fields is
himself deprived of the basic rights of feeding,
sheltering, and caring for his own family, the whole
community of man is sick.
— Cesar Chavez

A THLETICISM. Length. Power. Flexibility. Patience. Stamina. Aggression.

Am I talking about the qualities that NBA coaches are looking for in the next twelve-year-old basketball phenomenon? Nope. I'm talking about what it takes to cut it in the olive groves during the dry, hot August pruning in Tuscany.

The night we returned to *Barbialla Nuova* from Venice, Amy and Ken invited us to dinner with them and their friends Christian (Sardinian) and Hilly (South African) and their two kids. Dinner turned out to be a barbeque, Sardinian style, at an old hunters' outpost deep in the Tuscan wilderness. We hiked in at sunset, gathered some wood, lit a considerable fire and sat around and cooked on it for hours. (I learned a new barbecue trick that I can use on the beach. Yay.) If you've read

Farm Aid, then you can imagine what the meal and Prosecco and wine were like (wonderful). We listened to ghost stories and sang lullabies in Italian and Afrikaans—two beautiful and romantic languages—under a full moon and hiked out, exhausted, around midnight. Another fantastic experience that we won't soon duplicate or forget, courtesy of Ken and Amy.

We left our friends at *Barbialla* with heavy hearts (and semi-functioning livers) late last week, and spent the day riding bikes and eating (more) gelato around the lovely walled city of Lucca. Then we hopped in the Twingo for a ride to *Montecastelli*, our second WWOOF farm, which happens to be smack-dab in the middle of the Chianti wine region. We knew we were headed somewhere special when we turned off the rural highway on to a small paved road flanked by fields of sunflowers and vineyards.

Montecastelli did not disappoint.

The villa—it's not a "farm" in the conventional sense—sits atop a hill on an ancient road known as *La Francigena*. The 360-degree views are jaw-dropping all day but are really extraordinary at sunrise and sunset. Jens Schmidt and his family painstakingly restored the 1000-year old property over more than ten years.

To call it a triumph would be an understatement. The place is gorgeous and meticulously appointed, and Jens, who has called *Montecastelli* home for nearly twenty years, really knows the local food and wine and farm scene. He planted the 1200 tree olive grove in 1999 and handcrafts artisan olive oil. (He also raises pigs for his gourmet-in-every-sense-of-the-word prosciutto, which Wendi and I agree is the best we've had...ever.) If you're ever thinking "Tuscan villa vacation," then *Montecastelli* and Jens should be high on your list.

Perhaps unfortunately, we are not simply vacationing this time. We are WWOOFers, and thus working for our keep. We were given a class on pruning water shoots from olive trees to ensure their integrity and efficiency as they continue to mature (an approximately twenty-year process). It is hard work, real manual labor, under a Tuscan sun that has turned, ah, *warm*. (Close to "unbearably hot" during the middle of the day, so thank goodness for the swimming pool.)

We wake early to beat the heat and then put in a few hours in the evening too. We also help feed the pigs, donkeys and horses, and do some work in the garden. (The girls absolutely love this, and so do we.) We have a great apartment and continue to eat great meals, as you might imagine (we had a wild boar ragout that would have knocked your socks off; we're working on getting the recipe), and the local wines taste great in the late evenings. All is well.

I turned thirty-six last weekend.

We spent my birthday in Siena, yet another stunning Tuscan city. This one is the site of *Il Palio*, a wild horse race around the *Piazza del Campo* in which the jockeys—who ride bareback and are often tossed from their horses—are decked out in colorful uniforms representing their respective neighborhoods. The race dates back hundreds of years and bragging rights are significant, as can be seen from the flags all over the city bearing the winning neighborhood's colors.

We missed the race by a few weeks (bummer), but had lunch on the *Piazza*. Not only is it shocking that there is a bareback horse race in the oddly shaped and steeply canted plaza (not a conventional track by any stretch of the imagination), but it is truly shocking that the restaurant we lunched in could put out such a terrible meal.

That's right. We finally had a terrible meal in Tuscany.

Here we are, in the heart of one of the world's great food

and wine regions where beautiful ingredients are everywhere, and we were served overpriced dog food for lunch. It is a lesson we've learned before and will likely learn again: Beware the tourist trap. Find some place on a side street, even a street cart, that is crowded with people speaking the native language and let it rip. Nine times out of ten both your palate and your wallet will be pleasantly surprised.

After a nice time but disappointingly awful meal in Siena—it was really genuinely bad—we went back to *Montecastelli* to enjoy the sunset and had a great dinner (the aforementioned wild boar ragout) in the main courtyard. Wendi and I shared a cool bottle of a light white wine, the kids ran around and danced and played, we all sang happy birthday. It was a simple birthday, one to remember.

The next day, still in a celebratory mood, we drove a couple hours to the *Saturnia Hot Springs*, which were awesome. There were pools and rapids and waterfalls, all with water that's around eighty degrees. The place was packed with vacationing Italians, which added to the spectacle. (I'd never seen a Speedo that actually laces up the front. I digress.) We had a really good time and finished the day off with a fantastic meal in a small restaurant in a small town near *Montecastelli* that is off the beaten path.

After the kids went to bed, Wendi and I sat around and talked with Jens and his mother (she's here visiting) and his cousin (also visiting) and their friends over a bottle of wine. Once again, we found ourselves at a wonderfully mixed table, with German, Italian and English being spoken, everyone laughing and enjoying the company.

After Wendi fell asleep, I started thinking about my birthday and our present circumstances. Even just a year ago, I couldn't possibly have imagined that I'd turn thirty-six while working in an olive grove at a villa in Italy, while at the same time planning months of further travel with my wife and kids. I couldn't help but smile at life's inherent but all too often unacknowledged unpredictability and the new reality—even if only temporary—that we have created.

I also remembered that, when I was young, I thought that being twenty-five was "grown up." When I turned twenty-five, I thought, no, over thirty-five is more like it. And as I considered the question again, I realized that there is no denying it this time around. (Although I still *feel* like a kid.)

Then suddenly, as I drifted off to sleep, it struck me that I had finally and definitively answered the long-standing question of what, exactly, I would *be* when I grow up. (For those of you who know me and know of my constant search for an answer to this question, you'll appreciate the finality here.) All you have to do is look at my present employment.

I'm a migrant farm worker.

Viva la causa!

CHAPTER 16
FOOD FOR THOUGHT

San Gimingano, Italy
August 2011

I like food. Food tastes good.
—Descendents

I GUESS IT STARTED back in Dublin. We were walking to meet my family in their pub, *Sheehans*, when we stumbled across our first bright green "twin-tailed siren" logo just off of busy Grafton Street. It was surprising that it took so long, I suppose, even then.

"We shouldn't ever go into a Starbucks," I said to Wendi.

"Yeah, that's just like being back at home," she responded. "The whole point is to do the local thing."

We've not really discussed it since then but we have nevertheless purposefully, though not always easily (think crowded train stations, hungry kids, etc.), avoided Starbucks and McDonalds and KFC and Pizza Hut and other American chains. We have instead always hit local coffee houses and pubs and restaurants and dives—sometimes with less than stellar results (think *The Rotisserie Chicken Incident* and that dreadful meal in Siena) but most often with happy after-the-fact bellies—in an effort to be sure that we are all trying new foods and participating in the local cuisine and culture and drinking and dining scene.

This initially led us to such treasures as black pudding in Scotland (Wendi absolutely loved it until she was told how it was made in a graphic step-by-step gore-o-rama) and Andouillette Sausage in France (again, Wendi enjoyed it, sort of, until she better understood how it was prepared) and countless other dishes that we have all tried since embarking.

We have, of course, forced this upon our kids in an effort to ensure adequate … *exposure*. They are (loosely) required to at least attempt most everything, and if they do not like one thing or another, they are to be polite and say, "This is not for me, but [gratzie, merci, thanks, etc.]." They are most certainly *not* to say "yucky" or "icky" or "deeee-skusting" or anything of the sort.

Italy has been a proverbial picnic. Loads of lasagna, pounds of prosciutto, a plethora of pastas, rounds of risotto, countless variations of crème-filled delights. The kids have never eaten so much, or so well. I may have to start hunting and taking cooking classes when we get home to keep them going like this. Seriously.

The truth is that we have been generally successful with the whole "try new and interesting stuff" program and the kids are happily eating things they wouldn't have even looked at before we left. This has been relatively easy to date, of course, and we are banking on dividends come Africa or Asia. Only time will tell.

With that said, we have spent more than the past month in Tuscany, eating top-notch meals that would make any foodie envious. And our nearly four weeks in France were marked by budget-blowing breakfasts and lunches and dinners and snacks and treats and "once in a lifetimes" and, well, you get the idea. The truth is that Lily and Kate have no idea how lucky they've been. But we do.

And we hope that their little palates will develop accordingly.

Yet despite all of our efforts, one thing is absolutely clear. All the trying and liking and loving and rejecting and refusing (and arguing) have culminated in one clear food choice that trumps all others, beyond the shadow of a doubt. There is no reason to tempt fate, so we have chosen to let it slide over and over again. We have caved to the whims of a six-year-old and a three-year-old. And while we are wrestling with guilt and defeat and the skyrocketing cost of toothpaste, we are complicit.

Complicit indeed.

What's the food, you ask?

It's challenging to admit, but gelato is taking over our lives. We have it daily, sometimes even more frequently, and we all try new flavors and textures with reckless abandon. I had a lemon and grapefruit(!) double this afternoon and loved every creamy, delicious moment. I'd never have tried a grapefruit anything (save a Greyhound, I suppose) before getting to Italy, but they do something magical—*magical*, I tell you—with the ice cream here.

Maybe I'll try pistachio/blackberry/lemon tomorrow. Or Wendi could have *crema* with strawberry. Or maybe Lily wants to try mint with chocolate. Kate is always up for something new. Who knows what's next? In fact, maybe we should just go get some right now.

Whatever.

I guess we can wait until tomorrow to keep indulging our kids' gastronomic fantasies.

CHAPTER 17
THE STATE OF THE UNION

Rome, Italy
September 2011

---

*"And so, in my State of the—my State of the Union—
or State —my speech to the nation,
whatever you want to call it, speech to the nation—
I asked Americans to give 4,000 years—
4,000 hours over the next—the rest of your life—
of service to America.
That's what I asked—4,000 hours."*
—George W. Bush

I FELL FROM THE HIGH BRANCHES of an olive tree earlier this week. As I plummeted toward the surely unforgiving earth below, arms flailing and hands grasping for something, *anything*, that might help slow down the rapid escalation of speed brought on by that all too constant and often pesky gravitational pull, I did not see my life flash before my eyes. There were no hazy still photos of my wedding day or my daughters' births or my college graduation or anything else. Instead there was only a distinct and strong feeling of disbelief that I was a lawyer, sitting behind a desk all day every day, just less than twelve weeks ago.

We've been on the road since June 15. That's eighty days, if anyone is counting. Eighty-*one* days ago, we had a house, a business, classes and lessons for the girls, dinner dates with friends, the hustle and bustle of everyday life in California.

But all that changed on June 15.

Now we have only what we can carry, and we pretty much do what we want whenever it feels right. We have few obligations and those that we do have are typically self-imposed and pretty flexible. We have none of the stresses we once had, yet, anyway—there will be that bothersome reintroduction to real life to deal with at some point—and we've no meaningful worries.

We are tremendously free right now, man, and we are digging it.

Freedom is groovy.

And we are about to get even freer. We've reached the end of the "planned activities" portion of the trip, you see. We researched and studied and plotted everything we have done to date. From the apartment in Dublin and farm in west Cork to the road trip through Scotland to the week in Paris and the boat trip in Dijon to the organic farming work in Italy. All planned. All great. All done.

We spent the past month crisscrossing Tuscany, playing on its beaches and frolicking in the warm, gentle waters of the Etruscan Coast, working on its farms, meeting lots of locals and generally having a fantastic time. Jens Schmidt and his family really took us in at *Montecastelli* and treated us wonderfully. The work was hard, no doubt, but we were rewarded with a beautiful apartment, truly great meals (from roasted pigs' legs smothered in fresh rosemary and sage and garlic to fresh fish straight from the Mediterranean, from delightful salads right out of the massive garden to the creative and always terrific daily pasta lunches to whatever else Jens and the gang toted out of that magic kitchen), delicious wines and even *Montecastelli* t-shirts.

What a place.

Wendi and I will definitely return one day to check on the olive grove and take Jens up on some of his encyclopedic food and wine-related suggestions around Tuscany and beyond.

Mark my words.

We spent one day of our final weekend at *Montecastelli* just relaxing around the place, which says something. We spent the other day in Florence, truly the crown jewel of the Tuscan cities. We forced the kids into the *Uffizi*, which houses one of the world's great collections of Renaissance art, and had a simple requirement. Find the "top ten" works by Michelangelo, da Vinci, Raphael, Botticelli, etc. (and then we can get a gelato). Then we spent a few hours wandering the city and seeing the sites with Ken and Amy and their kids (our friends from *Barbialla Nuova*) before heading back to *Montecastelli* for the night. We had a blast and the kids all loved being back together. This will not be the last we see of Ken and Amy.

Again, mark my words.

So now what? With no real plans, what will we do? Will we be able to keep going? For how long? And to where? How are the girls (actually) doing? How are Wendi and I (actually) doing?

I'll take those questions in what seems to be the most logical order.

First, the girls are just fine; thriving, even. Lily is engaged and interested and eager to see more stuff and meet more people. She is devouring the *Magic Treehouse* literary series at an astonishing clip (she even understands it and takes tests and does related activities online!), and enjoys waking up before everybody else and lying in bed with the installment *du jour*. Believe it or not, she has started re-reading the initial books since we are presently out of new ones and haven't been able to find them on the road. (And the care package that was sent by Wendi's folks seems to have been lost in the mail, for now anyway.) She has taken on my slang—which is horrifying, of course—and sometimes says things like "Let's go chill out in the *piazza*," or, "That *limone gelato* was killer." She is surprisingly interested in cathedrals and religion, which is an interesting topic for a philosophy major to discuss with an inquisitive six-year-old in an ever-increasingly detailed fashion. She smiles a lot and loves and cares for her sister. She is wonderful and funny and smart and beautiful and cool to hang out with.

I love her dearly and couldn't be happier to share this time with her.

Kate is wild. Straight up. (In fact, she is singing *Edelweiss* and rolling around on the floor beside me here in Rome as I write.) She is constantly the subject of people's attention and is pretty into it, frankly. She likes Lily to read to her and is always enthusiastically striving to achieve all the things that Lily makes look so easy. She is really developing a little personality and unique way of doing things and seeing the world and it is amazing to watch her change on what seems to be a near daily basis. She is hilarious and often keeps crowds of people laughing and smiling as they wait in line for one thing or another. She is beautiful and wonderful and precocious and inquisitive and smart and also very cool to hang out with.

I love her dearly and love to spend my days and nights in her often wacky world.

Both girls have taken quite a liking to all things food-related. (Kate actually came to me the other night and told me that an imaginary friend was cooking octopus in garlic and white wine.) They like to set the table and serve the food and clear the table and help with the dishes. They pretend to sip wine and "cappuccinis" (not sure if that's good). They also like saying things in other languages and have mastered a few key phrases in French and Italian. Kate says she fluently speaks "kid language," and then goes into gibberish conversations with herself or Lily. They are funny and cute and they are good little sisters and friends.

Wendi is, well, Wendi is *Wendi*. Just like she has been since the day I met her. She is fun and easygoing and gorgeous and my companion and love. She doesn't know it but she is incredibly charming and makes traveling easy. I think I get more out of spending this time with her than she does with me and I couldn't imagine doing this with any other person. Really. And I can confidently say that she is happy and ready for more.

We have developed lots of family rituals or routines or whatever you want to call them, and they help remind us of our friends and family and make us feel at home wherever we are. For example, we light a candle for and talk about Bucky, our dog, every time we go into a cathedral. (That's quite a few euros donated to the churches here in Europe.) When things get tough, we play "big deal, small deal, medium deal," and that usually diffuses any ticking time bombs. We look through pictures of friends at home and talk about Santa Barbara and California and the United States.

We hold hands a lot.

We find little jokes or games nearly everywhere we go. We do our best to be courteous and kind and keep things light and fun. It's all good.

None of that is to say that the kids do not have their moments, as all three year olds and six year olds do. (For example, Lily sulked, arms crossed and brow furrowed, for at least twenty minutes after miscounting the *Spanish Steps*, and Kate had a Chernobyl-style I-stayed-out-too-late meltdown before bed last night after a wonderful evening at the *Pantheon*.)

Sometimes the tension and frustration that lives and breathes within those moments is amplified due to close living quarters or public places or whatever other condition that exists as a consequence of our travels. I think Wendi and I have been forced to take a closer look at our kids' behavior—good and not so good—and address it together, as more of a parenting team than ever. We let more slide but the kids seem more aware of which lines not to cross. We are one unit now, more than ever before, and we are together all the time. We do our best to treat each other with respect and dignity and courtesy and kindness, and we have been pretty successful in that regard. With that said, it isn't always a picnic and I am proud that we have made it this far and are still going strong.

———

As for me, well, I'm fine. I hit the ground hard but my fall from the olive tree left me with only a few scrapes and scratches and bruises. And as I stood up with the punk rock of my youth still playing loudly in the headphones in my ears, I looked around. And I saw the vineyards and the rolling hills and the sunflower fields and the olive groves of Tuscany stretched out before me. I switched the music off and listened to the wind in the trees and felt the sun hot on my face and bare chest. And I slowly realized that I had been down in the grove, alone, for hours and had long since passed quitting time.

I smiled.

And then I felt it. All of it. I felt surfing and mountain biking and snowboarding. I felt playing my guitar with old friends and all those things I once loved but eventually stopped doing for reasons that I no longer understand. I felt my friends and my family. I felt my kids. I felt my wife.

I laughed.

I found something out there in Jens's olive grove. Something that had been missing from my life for awhile but that had once guided me well for years. And while it culminated in the groves in Tuscany, it had roots in all that we've seen and done for the past few months. My family's pub in Dublin that they have owned for nearly 80 years. The vast fields and beauty of west Cork. Dougie the Scot building his place on Skye from the ground up and still going. The Parisians on Bastille Day. The Italians. The dedication of Ken and Amy to a particular way of doing and being. The commitment of Jens Schmidt to *Montecastelli* and all the truly wonderful things he creates there, and the drive he demonstrates on a daily basis toward his own perfection. The easy peace and happiness that each of these people exude.

Yeah, I found something out there in Jens's olive grove all right. I found passion. Passion for life and living, my way.

And I won't ever let it go again.

You can definitely mark those words.

We're not done yet. Not even close. So keep checking in and letting us know your thoughts and questions. We appreciate and value all the emails and notes and think of all of you as friends and participants in our travels. You make our experience richer, and we thank you for taking the time to peek in on our little world from time to time.

Peace and love.

PART TWO

FREE

You belong among the wildflowers;
You belong somewhere close to me.
Far away from your trouble and worry;
You belong somewhere you feel free.
—Tom Petty

CHAPTER 18
SIX-YEAR OLDS ARE GREAT GAMBLERS
AND OTHER LESSONS FROM THE ROAD

Bol, Island of Brac
Croatia
September 2011

Everything I learned in school, I learned again on the street.
—G. Love

THERE ARE PLENTY of rather obvious educational opportunities that stem from extended family travel—new languages, cultures, food, people etc.—but there are lots of other less conspicuous lessons out there, as well. On this trip alone, as those of you who have read this far know, I have learned that driving the winding, dipping country roads of west Cork at considerable velocity with a three-year-old strapped into the backseat only by lap-belt and thus without any real way to see the world rocketing by outside the car often leads to violent projectile vomiting. I've also learned to beware overcooked Parisian fowl, for they have a propensity to steal money right out of your wallet the moment you turn your back to find a bottle of wine. And I can now definitely say that French "adventure parks" are the equivalent of hell on earth and should be avoided at all cost.

Pretty straightforward stuff, frankly.

The past week has been an educational bonanza. Things just keep happening and I just keep having these "EUREKA!" moments. Some have been positive experiences and others, well, not so much. But all have taught me a few things that I will keep close for the rest of my life.

It Is Preferable to Avoid Dealing with the Police In Any Foreign Country

First of all, you really never want to have to deal with the police in any foreign country. Yeah, that's right, <u>any</u> foreign country. You just never know.

We left *Montecastelli* for Rome and were trying to figure out how to get on the freeway. Sounds simple but if you've driven in Italy, then you understand that's not always the case. We took a wrong turn and quickly realized that while we were getting on to the right freeway, we were headed north toward Denmark or Germany rather than south toward Rome. Our experience is that this simple mistake can lead to thirty minutes or more of recovery time and frustration, so we pulled off to the shoulder to evaluate our options.

It was immediately clear that a simple u-turn would solve all of our problems. It was also clear that the *Guardia di Finanza*—an Italian law enforcement agency that is primarily concerned with financial crimes and drug and other types of smuggling—was on the shoulder opposite us. The cops were out of their car, and seemed to be talking with another driver who was also pulled over.

They weren't even looking in our direction.

And we had seen literally hundreds of major and minor

traffic violations—the laws seem mere suggestions in Italy and are constantly broken—so we figured that a relatively safe u-turn with nobody around would be perfectly acceptable.

We were wrong.

This was one of those decisions I wanted back right after I made it.

The *Guardia di Finanza* literally jumped into the lane in front of me and pulled out a red, hand-held sign that said something like "pull over you moron, you just broke a simple traffic law directly in front of a relatively high ranking police officer." (It was in Italian, though, so I can't be sure.)

I eased the Twingo on to the shoulder.

I knew it was not great before the conversation even began. The officer was in his early forties and strutted toward us with an all-too-evident and rather large chip on his shoulder. It was clear that this was not just any beat cop, but an ITALIAN POLICE OFFICER who was tasked with UPHOLDING THE LAWS OF ITALY and took his job very seriously. I took my shades off, asked the perplexed children to please be quiet but polite if spoken to and rolled the window down.

The ITALIAN POLICE OFFICER removed his aviators (seriously) and glared down at me. He began speaking in his native tongue, fast, and I was able to make out only the very basics. He was asking me whether I made illegal u-turns like that in *France*. (The Twingo has French plates, so this was actually a reasonable question.)

I explained that I was not French.

The intensity of his glare grew stronger.

"What are you then?" he snarled in decent English.

"American," I said.

He did not hide his disgust. "Papers," he said dryly, and looked at my kids. "For everyone."

All of our passports and my international driver's license

were in the trunk, so I slowly opened the door and got out. He stopped me.

He looked me over from head to toe and sneered, right in my face, "We wear shoes when we drive in Italy." I was in fact barefoot but I had my Rainbows in the front seat. I grabbed them and slipped them on.

There are few words that might help describe the officer's reaction. His face twisted into a grotesque and hideous mask. He was conveying his hatred for me in a way that perhaps only an infuriated ITALIAN POLICE OFFICER could do.

"*Sneakers,*" he hissed. "We wear *sneakers* when we drive in Italy." (I can honestly say that I was not aware that the Italian government had gone so far as to regulate the specific variety of footwear its drivers must strap on before getting behind the wheel. But, again, I digress.) There was venom-spittle floating around him in the air.

I quickly gathered our papers and handed them over, reluctantly. He stormed away and began a private but excited conversation with his partner, who had been watching the whole scene unfold from afar while shuffling papers and doing other meaningless tasks in an effort to appear busy.

The dynamic duo spent the next half hour trying to figure out how to write me a ticket for my blunder. They asked for every single scrap of paper that reflected my ownership of the vehicle (we technically bought it under the Renault Eurodrive program and then sold it back when we were done with it after reaching Rome a few days ago) and made a half dozen calls or more checking on our paperwork and immigration status and who knows what else. I am absolutely 100% certain that he would have arrested me for any violation but our papers were in perfect order. There was nothing he could do.

He finally strutted back over to me, thrust the passports and other materials into my chest, looked me right in the eyes and barked out "BYE." Then he turned around and strutted away, sort of like a deflated peacock.

He never did figure out how to write me that ticket.

But that is beside the point. There is a tremendous amount of discomfort that flows from a foreign police officer's clear hatred and concurrent possession of your passport and other key documents. As the minutes passed, I became more and more concerned that he might just find something wrong, or say he found something wrong, with our papers. And what then?

I can't speak the language, my wife and kids are stuck in some French rental car with belligerent cops hassling them and me and we have no local accommodation or connection or friends. None of that is good and I was relieved when everything worked out.

So we have a new rule: Never do anything that might get you in hot water with the local fuzz.

It just ain't worth it.

Rome, by the way, is pretty mind-blowing and we really enjoyed it. From a *cappucco* at *Tazza d'Oro* to the *Vaticano* and the *Cappella Sistina* to the *Pantheon* and from the *Colosseo* to the *Piazzas di Spagna* and *Venezia* and *Navona* and the *Fontana di Treva* and on and on. Perhaps the single most mind-blowing thing of all is the vast wealth and property and artistic holdings of the church—it is truly unbelievable. Regardless, we've had a terrific time in Rome; even the girls have loved it, memorably playing glow-in-the-dark bouncy ball and giggling for hours at the *Pantheon*, where ancient Romans walked and talked and prayed to their gods nearly two thousand years ago.

Very cool.

Six-Year Olds Are Surprisingly Good Gambling Partners

After a few days in Rome, we took an overnight ferry from

the east coast of Italy (Ancona) to Croatia (Split). The boat was filled with retired Italians who were on holiday and wanted to party. It also had a night club and casino.

Uh-oh.

After we checked in and explored the boat a bit, we decided to sit outside and have a drink while the kids played. Simple and responsible. No problem.

But then these great Italians sat next to us and started in on the *"bellisima!"* and the cheek-pinching and we got to talking. And we had another beer. Cue more talking. Cue laughter and general merrymaking. Then they asked whether we would like some of *their* drink, which they had been pouring, in increasingly large amounts, from an old water bottle hidden in a brown bag. Intrigued, we said sure.

Whenever my wife says something like, "Yummy, this tastes like a lemon drop," look out. You are likely imbibing a very powerful alcoholic drink that has been significantly sweetened to mislead you about its potency. This was no exception.

After a couple rounds, we got up and hugged and kissed and eventually left our new friends.

Then I played roulette with Lily for a while.

I know, I know. But before you pass judgment, consider this. There was another kid at the table. And Lily learned a lot about working with numbers and quickly became adept at simple subtraction. She actually picked up the basics pretty fast.

It was like homeschool.

Yeah, it was just like homeschool.

Here's the great thing about gambling with a six-year-old. There's no fear. No fear of mounting losses, no fear of a disappointed wife or mother. There is only unbridled excitement for the next bet or the next win. And there is a limitless supply of optimism. We were high-fiving and laughing and causing a scene. She loved it. And even though we lost a few euros, so did I.

After we put Wendi and Kate to bed with the chess board and Italian chocolate we subsequently decided to purchase (duty free!), I asked Lily if she was ready for sleep. I won't forget her response:

"Let's go party, daddy."

She's her father's daughter. (And her mother's daughter, frankly.)

We went up to the top deck and split a coke. We looked out over the Adriatic Sea, searching in vain for land, and talked about surfing and the stars and our friends and my travels before this trip. We went to the night club and danced to the sounds of a comically-stoic Croatian pianist playing everything from waltzes to American rock and roll covers. (Lily's favorite was *Rock Around the Clock*. Trust me, it was hilarious.) Sometimes people were dancing, though mostly ballroom-type stuff, and sometimes we were out there alone. We slow danced and fast danced and foot danced and belly danced and probably made quite a spectacle. When we finally left the floor at around 11:00 pm, a group of people in the back gave us a standing ovation. Lily was thrilled.

And she wanted to do one last thing before bed. There were a few areas of the boat that were designated for "kissing" and she was interested. (She can read all these pesky signs now, so it is becoming harder to hide the real world from her.) Against my better judgment, we headed to the back of the boat where, thankfully, there was nobody but us. We sat down, gave each a quick hug and a kiss and talked and giggled a bit more before hitting the sack.

I wish she'd stay six forever, man. I'm just not sure how she'd be received at a craps table in Vegas.

Having No Travel Plan Is, Well, It's Really Good

We landed in Croatia the next morning and immediately got into the Split beach scene. Let me put it to you this way, I was served a delicious and cold local beer, in a heavy glass beer stein, while sitting on a lounge chair with my feet in the sand just a few feet from the warm, crystal clear sea.

At 9:30 in the morning.

Perfectly appropriate. The kids swam and played in the sand for hours. Wendi barely moved. We did the same thing the next day, with a few minor adjustments.

When we finally decided to start looking at how best to get to Greece from Croatia and when to go (we were in no hurry), we realized that we made a small travel blunder. Geographically speaking, movement between the two countries should be a no-brainer. But things have changed quite a bit in this region over the past fifteen or twenty years and it is not as easy as you might expect. The options are basically (1) a 20 hour, multi-faceted bus ride through Albania, or, perhaps, Bosnia and Herzegovina, with unreliable connections, (2) a very expensive flight or (3) an overnight ferry back to Italy followed by another one to Greece. No great choice economically or otherwise. We were stuck, sort of, and must now work on a way out at some point.

Some might view this as a problem that comes from traveling without any real plan.

But we know better. We believe a little patience will pay off here and that our path will soon become obvious. So we decided to head out to the idyllic islands off Split to figure it out. Guess we'll have to stay put for a while.

Bummer.

CHAPTER 19
MANGO FARM

Bol, Island of Brac
Croatia
September 2011

When the world gets crazy
We can go to Mexico and live
On the beach with monkeys and bananas and pineapples
Fish are swimming in the deep blue sea
Next to our Mango Farm.
— Spencer the Gardner
(aka *The Organic Gangster*)

I HAVE A CLOSE FRIEND named Sam. Sam and I have a joke. But it's more than a joke, really, it's a dream that we share. It comes up every time we see each other, over drinks or at the beach or with the kids. (It used to come up a lot when we surfed together.) It's real and it's happy and it's good and I love it.

It's a mango farm. That's right, a *mango farm*.

Our mango farm is not just a physical location, it's a whole way of life and of living and being. It's some place warm, near a beach, where we can go with our wives and our kids and be together, away from the rigid schedules and constant hassles of everyday life. Away from technology and television and advertisements and cell phones and other distractions. It's a place where the food and drink are healthy and delicious, the people are kind and generous and there is a sense of community and caring. There are no worries or stresses that can't be addressed quickly and easily, and there is no complaining or whining. There is just peace and quiet and family and friends and surf and love.

And there are mangos, of course. Lots of mangos that we can eat or sell or use for salsa or cocktails or whatever. Very important.

I used to know this was all a fantasy. I used to know that there are no places where people are that nice and life is that easy and mangos are that plentiful. And I knew that if there were ever any places like that, they were found and exploited long ago and no longer exist.

But I'm not so sure anymore.

We've been in Bol on the Croatian Island of *Brac* for well over a week now and are having a hard time leaving. We were supposed to be here for three days, then five, then seven. But we haven't been able to go. The weather is perfect. The water is warm and healing and rejuvenating. The people are hospitable. The food is fresh and simple and wonderful. The beaches are immaculate. The vistas are masterpieces; you can almost see the brushstrokes. And all of it is backed by beautiful mountains and trails and hiking and biking (think Tahoe in the summer time, with all of its smells and sights and beauty).

Wendi and I keep reminding each other that this isn't real, that no place could be so perfect. But it is real. We have the dark tanned skin and salty bleached-out hair and full bellies and rested souls to prove it. In fact, I'll bet you a *Karlovacko* (delicious local beer) that our collective aggregate heart rate isn't more than sixteen beats per minute.

Go ahead, test us.

There's a beach here, called *Zlatni Rat*, and it is unlike any I have seen. It is a long finger-like protrusion of sand and pine trees and happy people that extends out into the Adriatic Sea. One side is perfect in the mornings, warm and calm with crystal clear turquoise waters. The other side is perfect once the local breeze kicks up, protected by and smelling of the pine trees nearby. Its waters stay perfectly calm and clear all afternoon. Then you can switch back to the first side in the evenings, when the breeze dies, to watch the sun sink slowly into the sea. There are restaurants and bars in the middle of the peninsula, under the pines, that keep you full and relaxed all day.

It's a special place, man. A very special place indeed.

And, perhaps not surprisingly, it was there at *Zlatni Rat* that we met Andrew and Diana and their young daughter, Mia, from Seattle and their good friend, Paul, from San Diego. Diana heard Lily and Kate playing in the water, speaking English, and walked over to introduce Mia to the girls and say hello. That began a conversation that lasted for six hours in waist deep water with the girls splashing and swimming and giggling around us.

Beer was consumed. A quick and easy friendship was born.

Our new friends invited us to dinner in town and we accepted. It turns out that Diana is Croatian—her parents are actually from *Brac*—and speaks the language fluently. It also turns out that she is the cousin of a former world-class Croatian water polo player who is something of a national hero, having helped secure a gold medal for the country and having been ranked the world's top player a number of years ago. This type of thing is taken seriously here, and Diana (pronounced "Dee-ana") is treated quite well.

Dinner was spectacular. A beautiful restaurant right on the water, sun setting, great conversation, kids happy. Josep, the restaurant's owner and chef, came to the table bearing his own wine made from his own grapes grown on the island (delightful) and platters of grilled meats and fish and shellfish and bowls of salad made from fresh local produce drizzled with locally crafted olive oil and who knows what else. I was in heaven, an eating and drinking bliss-trance, and frankly don't remember everything we tasted or nibbled or gobbled or guzzled.

We finished the meal off with *raki*—maybe the most unique and powerful liquor I've tasted (and I've tasted a few)—and the rest of the night is a happy blur. I do know that we all made it home just fine and slept well. Good times, to be sure.

And they got even better.

We woke up the next morning and went to meet Andrew, Diana, Mia and Paul—who my kids had begun calling "Uncle Paulie" the night before (hmmm, not sure)—for a day on Josep's boat, exploring a couple islands and generally relaxing. We loaded up with snacks and beverages and jumped on board. An hour later we were on the more remote island of *Vis*, and spent another hour exploring its main town and having lunch and ice cream and fun.

Then we were back on the boat, heading for an even further and smaller island, *Bisevo*, and a well-known tourist attraction called the *Blue Cave*.

I'll take a stab at painting the scene.

We pull into a small bay with emerald waters of endless clarity. The bay is surrounded by high cliffs, and there is really nothing but a small bar on the water with cold beers and charcuterie and ice cream. So there's something for everybody and I am personally in a very good place. In fact, I am so happy that I don't even really care to go see this *Blue Cave*. I could hang out at the mooring all day, swimming and laughing and playing with the kids. No problem.

But then Josep, who seems to know everybody everywhere

we go, comes over and announces, with a bright smile on his face and beer in his hand, "It is time to go to the cave, now." He had arranged for a private viewing, and the gawking tourists had been cleared out of our way. This was Josep, unendingly generous with his time and hospitality and a truly great guy (and a good boat captain, too).

We get on a small boat to take us over to the cave and everybody is excited. After motoring through a few tight spots, we slow and enter an impossibly small crack in the side of a large rock outcropping that requires ducked heads and a lack of claustrophobia. It is dark. But then, suddenly, we round a dimly lit corner and find an open cathedral of rock and water.

It is positively mind-blowing.

Sunlight can only enter the cave through the water underneath one of the cliff walls, some 30 feet under the surface. The crystal clear water actually glows, as do the walls and ceiling that frame it. *Lunar* is one word that comes to mind. *Other-worldly* is another.

It's an awesome place, and we had it to ourselves.

Unfortunately, you aren't permitted to swim in it. But *we* were. Josep arranged that too.

It is a wild place, the *Blue Cave*, and we spent lots of time frolicking about in its waters amongst new friends. Amazing.

And that wasn't it. Josep, it turned out, had one more trick up his sleeve. He drove us back over to *Brac* but, rather than heading home, he took us to a boat-in only restaurant owned by some friends on a seaside cliff topped with vineyards and olive groves. The owner was literally pulling our dinner out of the Adriatic as we moored. Then he picked us up in his skiff and took us to the dock.

We spent the next few hours feasting, *feasting*, I tell you, on squid-ink risotto—incredibly sweet and rich and wonderful—and whole fish cooked over cherry wood coals with local olive oil and salt. (That was all it needed.) I got my hands on one of the cheeks over Uncle Paulie's stern objection and there was nothing but a fish skeleton straight out of a Tom and Jerry cartoon at the end. The whole thing was washed down with obscene amounts of locally produced white wine (with sparkling water) and, eventually, a Turkish coffee. I think most of us dozed on the boat ride back to Bol.

I know I did.

The next day, we rented a car and drove across the island through a few ancient Balkan villages to meet some friends from Santa Barbara—Jeff, his son Mateus and his crew and friend Roland—who happened to be cruising the nearby islands. (I love serendipity; this was not planned and seems impossibly unlikely as I write now.)

They had sailed from Turkey, where Jeff parks his (beautiful) boat, and were on the last leg of the trip to stow it further north for the winter. Jeff picked us up on the skiff and we spent the day sailing and swimming in gorgeous waters. Then he took us to lunch at yet another boat-in only restaurant on yet another unnamed small island serving fresh local fish that the server brought to the table, whole and raw, to show us before grilling. Another feast, this one of fresh local prawns and fish, grilled, with local white wine. Wonderful food, wonderful company. We finished it off with *grappa* and honey and a couple pancakes for the girls.

Jeff and the gang even thought of Kate's birthday—she turned four today—and provided her first gift, a small donkey figurine with packs and a bell and a sign around its neck that reads "I love Croatia." Then Kate was treated to Happy Birthday in English and Portuguese and Spanish and Croatian. Truly a treat of a day.

In between boating adventures with friends new and old, we spent days floating through time. We sat on one beach or another (at the other end of town, there is a mellow but gorgeous stretch right next to an ancient monastery that we really dug), we cooked great dinners, we played chess over cappuccinos in beachside cafes (yes, Lily is learning to play chess and she is stoked on it, which, in turn, makes me, a closet chess junkie, stoked too), we devoured wonderful local pastries (including a cheesy, sourdoughy, flaky super pastry that I cannot stop inhaling, sometimes with jam, sometimes straight up), we wandered through town and its narrow stone alleys, going for the occasional swim or run.

We cruised.

Truth be told, I can't tell you exactly what happened and when during that period; Bol is just that kind of place. Time didn't stop here—there are modern conveniences and a cool little village that has everything you need—but time is completely irrelevant here. You eat when you're hungry. You drink when you're thirsty. You jump in the water when you're warm. You sleep when you're tired.

It's a wonderful place.

But there are two problems. One is the total lack of mangos. You could probably make up for that deficiency with wine grapes or olives, but mangos are indeed important to the Mango Farm Ideal and their absence cannot be overstated.

The second problem is the lack of surf, which is undeniable. But with an individual resting heart rate of around four beats per minute and all the other great stuff happening here (including tons of windsurfing, kite boarding and mountain biking), you may be able to get past it.

Maybe.

We found it, Sammy, almost. My eyes are open man. *Mango farm is real.* It does exist.

And we are going to find it.

CHAPTER 20
A FAST CHANGING WORLD

Istanbul, Turkey
September 2011

Toto, I have a feeling we're not in Kansas anymore.
—Dorothy Gale

O UR PLANE FROM ISTANBUL took off late and landed even
later at a small rural airport in *Kayseri* in central Turkey.
By the time we collected our bags and made it to the shuttle
that would carry us to *Goreme* in Cappadocia, it was already
dark and we had been told that there was nearly an hour
drive ahead of us.

Then the ancient Mercedes van wouldn't start.

Communication with our seemingly nervous driver was
impossible so there was little understanding on our part of
what might happen next. (Never the most comforting feeling
when you're a long way from civilization in a totally new and
faraway place with two young daughters.) When the beast
miraculously coughed and gurgled and spat its way to life, we
took off quickly and rocketed over bad roads through a desolate
desert wilderness under a ceiling of stars that looked different,
somehow, than the one in California. It was a peaceful ride,

hypnotic even, and we all simply watched an alien landscape pass out the window.

It was near eleven when the van broke down again. We took it in stride, as we have learned to do, and piled ourselves and our things on the side of some road that was quite literally in the middle of nowhere. As we stood alone in the cold and damp night, examining the strange stone and sand configurations around us—some with almost human shapes lit by a bright moon that cast shadows with a propensity to play tricks standing mysterious against an oily black sky—we slowly realized that these strange sculptures were riddled with clearly man-made openings and markings.

People lived here, once, and maybe still.

An uneasy silence fell upon us.

That silence was broken, suddenly, by *Adhan*, the Islamic call to prayer. Although the call comes from mosques around five times a day over loudspeakers affixed to towering *minarets*, it was a shock out there in the desert where it seemed to come from nowhere, or everywhere, all at once. To say we were startled would be the understatement of the century.

The call is haunting; a man's voice singing in a foreign tongue and unfamiliar rhythms and tones. In this particular case, it actually raised the hair on my neck. Wendi and I looked at each other over the girls and although no words were spoken, it was clear that we were thinking the same thing.

We are a long, long way from the beaches and cocktail parties of Santa Barbara.

—•—

We (finally) left Croatia after celebrating Kate's fourth birthday doing basically whatever she wanted on *Brac*. Most of whatever she wanted after nearly two weeks on the island was to spend as much time floating around on a paddleboat with a water slide stuck on top of it as possible. She and Lily may have set a Croatian record for number of slides attempted and completed in one day. Then we had a dinner (and desert!) of Kate's choosing and the girls went to sleep happy.

Wendi and I stayed up late marveling at the fact that our kids are now six and four, and at how fast those years have gone. They've been good years, and we hope for many (many) more.

We left as the sun rose the next morning and were treated to a beautiful ferry ride back to Split. Then a few hours in a café on the waterfront with all our stuff, then a cab to the airport, then a plane ride to Budapest, where we had a seven hour layover before getting on a second plane, this one bound for Istanbul.

It was a long travel day for all of us—especially Lily and Kate—but we were excited to reach Turkey, which is not only an important place for us from a traveling-degree-of-interest perspective but from a symbolic one, too.

We've suddenly come a long way, man. A long way indeed.

Incidentally, we took the opportunity provided by the (excruciatingly long) layover in Budapest to have a quick dinner and roam a few streets on the *Danube*. Dinner was really good—I had a delicious Hungarian goulash followed by deer with cranberry sauce and Wendi had a game stew that she enjoyed until she bit into a small piece of glass in her last bite (darn!)—and the areas surrounding the river are vibrant and beautiful, with tons of restaurants and bars and shops and people. We put it on the "places we would like to see or spend more time in the next time we travel around the world" list, and would easily recommend a few days there to anybody based on our three (ok, four) hour tour, for what it's worth.

We left Budapest and landed in Istanbul at 3am. The kids were walking zombies—zombies that were predisposed to cry for any or no reason at all—and Wendi and I were *tired*.

(Enough said.) We stumbled through the gigantic and basically empty airport, figured out a visa issue that should have been easier than it was and then pushed our way through what felt like miles of roped-off lines designed to accommodate thousands of eager foreign visitors awaiting their turn at the passport control and customs area. We were literally the only people in the place, and the whole thing felt surreal in our sleep deprived state, almost like we had been institutionalized in light of the shiny white tile and walls gleaming around us.

Still, we smiled. For we knew that we would soon be comfortable in the house of friends.

Kami and Casey are Californians from Manhattan Beach who moved to Istanbul a few months ago. Kami is a Turkish citizen and his father has a very interesting business in Istanbul that required some help. He also happens to be one of the funniest people I know and I have always really enjoyed hanging out with him. Casey is similarly funny and easy going and affirmatively responded to Kami's plea for marriage, so they are here together, indefinitely. They are tremendously hospitable and welcoming, and we were thrilled to be staying at their place for a few days.

We woke up late the next morning after just a few hours of sleep and were treated to "a day of villages," as Casey explained. We started in Kami and Casey's new hometown, *Yesilkoy*, where we had a lovely traditional Turkish breakfast with tea in a park teeming with peacocks and ducks and chickens and people with a great view of the Marmara Sea. Then we strolled down a cool street in *Bakirkoy* and shopped (Casey deftly led us to books in English) and gobbled some delicious Turkish street food. Full and still a bit tired from the night before, we jumped on a ferry that crossed the Marmara from the European side of Istanbul to the Asian and stole a few precious minutes of shut-eye before landing in *Kadikoy*, where we wandered a bustling fish market and tasted mounds of fantastic Turkish finger foods.

We stopped for a long late lunch over a bottle of *raki*—I haven't been able to get away from the stuff since Croatia—and indulged in all sorts of new dishes and flavors that everybody really enjoyed. Kami is fluent in the language and the cuisine of Turkey (and Casey is full of knowledge herself after only four months here), so we really had a great time and learned and tasted a lot.

We got back to the apartment a bit late and got the (completely exhausted) children to bed. Then Kami and I played backgammon on his deck for a few hours. If asked under oath I would likely plead the fifth, but I feel comfortable admitting here that there was at least some additional *raki* involved. (Like I said, I just can't get away from the stuff.) I'm pretty sure that we ended in a dead heat, two games apiece, when the *raki* disappeared and the dice went mysteriously missing.

We (mercifully) started late again the next day and celebrated Wendi and my seventh wedding anniversary with a traditional *Kehvalti* breakfast prepared by Casey. (She has a culinary degree, need I say more?) Then we drove down to the *Bosphorus* and had a snack and Turkish coffee on the water before taking an hour cruise on the beautiful waterway that ultimately connects the Mediterranean to the Black Sea and is flanked by Europe on one side and Asia on the other. Very cool.

We followed that up with more street food and general wandering and people watching in busy *Taksim Square*, which was quite a lesson in population density. Casey promised an anniversary gift—a hidden oasis in the middle of all that chaos—and steered us to a secret lemon garden wedged between some buildings on a side street of a side street. We were treated to much-deserved and delicious sweet lemon and mint infused cocktails (virgins for the girls, of course; just because Lily played roulette doesn't mean we are letting her drink too.) It was a unique anniversary that we really enjoyed, and we were glad to spend it with friends and the kids.

We spent the next day wandering the spice market, which was great. Lily and Kate drew a fair amount of attention from the shop keepers and others, and loved all the colorful and fragrant spices and *Turkish Delight* candies and watching the homing pigeons fly away and return and petting the bunnies and puppies and everything else that was there. So did Wendi and I.

The fact is that Kami and Casey spoiled us. We saw a side of Istanbul that few tourists see, and we did it in the company of a couple very cool folks backed by the security and comfort of their knowledge and home. Perhaps it is best to say that staying with them was a big deal for us and we owe them a debt of gratitude (or more), even if they wouldn't accept it.

We left Kami and Casey to spend a few days in Cappadocia, which, despite our aforementioned ill-fated shuttle ride, was pretty mind-blowing. The place is visually insane. It looks like a massive giant spent centuries building drip-style sand castles, squeezing wet sand through his (or her) hands resulting in wax-like configurations that are truly out of this world. We spent our days there exploring the very caves that seemed so ominous in the middle of the night on that remote stretch of road and wandering through ancient underground cities that early Christians used as hiding places in times of persecution or war.

By the way, these cities really are underground—some going as deep as eight stories down—and are very cool (some even had rooms designated as wineries; gotta love those Christians!). We crawled through deep, dark passageways and found secret rooms. We saw some unbelievably well-preserved Christian art painted directly on cave walls that was beautiful and different than anything we've seen to date. Even Lily and Kate seemed to grasp the significance and meaning of these places, and they begged to go through them again and again. We obliged and all involved had a hell of a good time.

Speaking of good times, we bit the proverbial bullet and took our kids to a dinner show that promised lots of Turkish culture in the form of dining and dancing. We had already done very well with Kami and Casey and on our own, I think, on the dining front, but the dancing was new and the girls were excited to see exactly what people meant by this "whirling dervish" dance.

We have done these types of things before, though not often. In Hawaii, for example, we saw some pre-packaged show involving hula-ing and fire-twirling and tribal dancing and whatever else, over a "traditional" meal that was poorly conceived and executed.

So let's just say that our expectations were not particularly high.

But we were pleasantly surprised with decent food and a "touristy" but fun show. Kate was deathly afraid of the dervish dancers before they started whirling (there is a pre-whirling religious ritual that traditionally takes place under black lights, apparently, and is set to eerie music—eerie to a four year old kid from California, anyway—and she kept repeating, "Don't let those men dance over here, daddy," before she ran for the sanctuary that is Wendi's lap), but she warmed up eventually.

After the dervish twirling finale, there was a healthy serving of *raki*—I just can't get away from the stuff—followed by a whole dancing extravaganza that seemed to be the story of a Turkish wedding. Kate and Lily were both repeatedly chosen to participate and did so, eagerly (which means I did too).

At one point, with Kate on my shoulders, we actually *conga-ed* our way up some stone passageway to a massive bonfire, where there was more *raki*—the stuff follows me everywhere, I swear—and dancing with a drunken cross-set of humanity from all corners of the globe. (I'm not exactly sure of the precise moment in history when the conga-line was introduced to the ancient Turks, but it was fun nonetheless.) Some belly dancing was even thrown in at the end of the show for good measure. Good times.

We spent another day visiting Avanos, which is actually a pretty modern city (BMWs and Mercedes would occasionally roll past us) that is well-known for its ceramics and pottery. Both Lily and Kate had a quick lesson and got to throw a coffee mug and wine goblet, respectively. Again, a blast. (All except for that frankly bizarre haircut I accidentally got. Sort of the neo-gay Turk. Interesting for sure.)

In fact, our whole experience in Turkey has been fantastic and we have met many people who are not just kind and interesting but who are also interested in us (and America and Americans, frankly) and who we are and what we are doing. The Turks' profound and seemingly endless and very real love for Lily and Kate has only amplified the experience. We thought that the Italians couldn't be rivaled but not a block goes past here without somebody picking the girls up or kissing them or pinching their cheeks and tousling their hair and striking up a conversation in simple English with them (and usually but not always with us). It can be a bit aggressive, even bordering on inappropriately rough at times, but we are careful and polite with boundaries and the girls laugh and play into it, having a ball.

Indeed, these Turks seem to be genuinely all about kids and family. My feeling is that there are not zillions of young blond kids from California running around Istanbul or Cappadocia all the time, so Lily and Kate are something new and different and interesting. (They are also very cute. I know, I'm biased.

Whatever.) The whole thing is a lot of fun, and often leads to a piece of candy or some other treat so the kids are thrilled.

I've even had one or two beers bought for me, so who am I to complain?

———•———

We are back in Istanbul now and staying in an apartment in *Sultanahmet*, a really vibrant area near the city's most well-known sites. We had an amazing breakfast this morning in the shadow of the *Blue Mosque* and *Aya Sofia*. The self-described Arab in white robes sitting next to us smoking a Turkish *nargile* (probably better known as a *hooka*) secretly sent a specially-delivered order of delicious *baklava* to our table for the kids. Another real treat.

After breakfast we explored *Aya Sofia*, which has been, perhaps surprisingly, a church *and* a mosque at various times throughout its near 1500 year history. (It is a museum now.) Being in such a rich and beautiful place, surrounded by people from every walk of life—some with heads and shoulders covered by scarves, others fully covered by dark flowing *burqas*, and still others in familiar western dress—forces one to consider at least some of life's big issues.

It is absolutely clear that the world is changing fast around us now, and there are obvious differences between our family and those amongst whom we walk and talk and eat and sleep. Different colors, shapes, cultures, foods, styles of dress, mannerisms, languages, religions and philosophies are everywhere.

But standing in the grandeur of *Aya Sofia*, I realized that these differences are mostly all purely superficial, and that in many ways—the most important ways—we are all really the same (except for the few outlying anomalies that are always, and sometimes rightfully, the focus of so much attention). We all do our best to raise our kids. We all try to do the right thing as often as possible. We'd all like to leave a positive mark on the world that our children will live in long after we are gone. We all believe in something. We all build enormous temples and pray to the gods that have meaning to us. We all suffer sometimes. We all want a better life sometimes too.

And I thought of all the people here in Turkey kissing my kids and laughing and smiling and playing with them. These kind and generous people—just like the vast majority of their American and European and Asian and African and Latin counterparts—are the same ones who we read about in the news as (arbitrarily) being injured or dying in senseless struggles for power or money or religion that have little or no meaning to regular people who just want to keep their kids and those close to them safe and happy.

That simple, seemingly obvious realization was a hard pill—an emotional pill—for me to swallow. *They* are *us*, my friends, and *we* are *they*. There is no way around that fact when you are here, on the ground, amongst at least some of the *thems*. I can't think of a more important lesson for Lily and Kate to learn, and even if that and nothing else comes from this experience then it will have been one of the great successes of my life.

After *Aya Sofia* we leisurely strolled through *Sultanahmet Park* to the *Blue Mosque*. Wendi and the girls donned scarves to cover their heads and shoulders and we all took our shoes off and slowly walked barefoot alongside the devout through their house of worship and the tombs of Sultans long since passed. There were literally hundreds of people in the main section of the mosque but the girls were singled out of the crowd and invited into an area that was off limits to everybody except for one or two praying Muslims.

They walked away from us with two fully-covered friendly Muslim women and returned a few moments later, beaming.

As we left through the outer doors of the mosque, *Adhan*, the call to prayer, filled the air all around us. And this time, it sounded different than it did out there in the desert near Cappadocia.

It sounded beautiful.

Respect. Understanding. Peace. Love.

To everybody.

CHAPTER 21
TURKISH DELIGHT (FOR ADULTS ONLY)

Istanbul, Turkey
September 2011

Max, can you earmuff it for me?
—Bernard "Beanie" Campbell

IT GOES WITHOUT SAYING that there are many experiences—whether at home or abroad—that are not perfectly appropriate for children. And it is fair to say that we, as adults, sometimes find it difficult to pass up some of those experiential opportunities just because the kiddies are around. This proves especially true when you are traveling through places to which you may never return and that provide unique offerings, and you are with your kids all day long every single day. Trust me.

Our trip is all about new experiences in new places for the kids, of course, but for Wendi and me too. So we long ago decided not to forego absolutely everything that may not be rated G. We decided to indulge, when and where appropriate, in at least some of the more interesting things that come our way.

And that is precisely how I came to pay eighty lira to be assaulted by two very large Turkish men in a *hamam* in Istanbul.

Yes indeed, a day at the Turkish bath is quite an experience. Whereas you might pay hundreds of dollars (or more) to wear luxurious bath robes and slippers, drink mint and cucumber-infused mineral water and be generally pampered by beautiful women (or men, as the case may be) at some chic place in the Napa Valley, here at the *hamam* you pay the equivalent of around $45 to wear a small kilt-like piece of cloth—which is more like a cross between a durable tablecloth and an adolescent private school girl's skirt than it is sensuous bathwear—and get mugged, for lack of a better word, by a couple enormous Turks.

It's an interesting interpretation of the "spa day," for sure, but it has been around in one form or another since the time of the Greeks so they must be doing something right.

My day at the *hamam* began with an ancient woman who, through a series of jerky hand gestures and impatient grunts, directed me to undress and put my plaid miniskirt on. Easy enough in the small changing area reminiscent of a doctor's examination room, but you cannot stay there. And there is no locker room or staging area to which you might retire to spend a few moments listening to Enya by a fire. There is only the reception area with random gawkers (perverts?), customers and vendors wandering through at any given time. It also opens directly to the crowded street so there is a constant stream of people from all over the globe admiring your figure in women's clothing.

Not exactly the Napa ambiance.

(Note that I had chosen this particular bath house because it was billed as a largely genuine experience instead of a more sanitized, "yuppified" version offered at many of the high-end hotels in the area. I thought this was a good thing, but it is now very clear to me that I would have had a far different experience at the *Four Seasons* down the street.

After a fairly awkward few minutes of standing around in my skirt pretending to appreciate the faded pictures on the reception area walls, I was instructed to follow a male attendant. So I did.

He took me into the bowels of the place, and eventually to a massive sauna punctuated by large marble tables and what appeared to be wash basins on the walls. Like his colleagues in the reception area, he spoke no English but eventually made clear that he expected me to lie down on a gigantic slab of marble in one wing of the steam room. Again submissive, I complied.

The heat in the place was gentle but relentless. The marble was wet and downright hot, and I was sweating profusely within a few minutes of lying down. Directly above me was a huge rock dome, maybe thirty or forty feet high and three feet thick. It had been painted long ago, and its green and yellow hues were now very dull and very thin, revealing a layer cake of additional thin and faded colors from paint jobs of the (probably very distant) past all the way down to bare rock. Twenty-three cylinders (I counted them myself) had been cut through the rock to permit light and fresh air to enter the room. Some had been capped with colored glass, resulting in vibrant tubes of sunlight streaming down through the water vapor high in the dome.

It was hypnotic there, laying on my back in that all-encompassing heat, looking up into the belly of a kaleidoscopic dome that seemed centuries old. Voices speaking in unfamiliar tongues occasionally drifted softly through the sauna, echoing off the marble and the rock, inducing sleep. My eyelids grew heavy. I happily floated in and out of consciousness.

It was thus all the more startling when I was awoken by an enormous Turkish man standing above me in nothing but a skirt like mine. I use "enormous" appropriately in this instance to describe a mountain of a man, no shorter than six-foot-five and no lighter than 300 pounds. He towered over me, making hand signals and grunting like a cave man. In a plaid miniskirt. Nothing else.

It took me a second in my dazed and confused state but I eventually gathered that he wanted me to move, so I staggered to my feet. He pointed to a wash basin that he had apparently filled for me and pushed a shallow bucket in my chest. "Clean," he said, and walked away. I wasn't totally sure what to do, but began filling up the bucket he gave me from the larger basin and pouring it over my head and shoulders, further soaking my now thoroughly drenched skirt. Nobody objected (I was alone, though, so maybe that wasn't the greatest indication of proper conduct) so I repeated filling and dumping until the basin was empty. The mechanical repetition and weight of each fairly large bucket combined with the warm water and ever-present heat to drop me back into the desired state of semi-consciousness.

But things changed pretty quickly from there. The 300-pound man returned, this time with a white oven-mitt and scrub-brush that may at one time have been used to clean barnacles off of old boats. (Bad sign.) He grunted, pointing to a larger marble table in the center of the room. I was a bit reluctant but kept thinking that lots of people—Turkish and otherwise—do this all the time, so who am I to refuse?

I laid face down on the table and awaited my fate.

He started by pouring gallon after gallon of near scalding water over me, from head to foot and then from foot to head. Okay, all right...that was basically good once my brain communicated to my body that I was not going to lose layer after layer of skin due to significant burning. Pretty relaxing, actually.

Then he strapped on his oven mitt.

Now I am open to pretty much anything and not much bothers me. (In the words of Ben Harper, "if you're causing no harm, you're all right with me.") With that said, *relaxed* would not be the term to accurately depict either my mental or physical state at this point. *Seriously concerned* and *tensed up tightly* would be more appropriate.

The next fifteen minutes was marked by him violently scrubbing every inch of my body—except those covered by my now soaked cocktail napkin-sized kilt—with the rough glove he donned. After the first few "gentle" strokes, he really put his weight and strength into it, effectively sanding off layer after layer of my skin—the very skin I was thrilled to still have post-scalding water soak—in an exercise of extreme exfoliation, for sure. He alternatively sang in Turkish and grunted and groaned as he pressed hard on my comparatively puny frame. (I kept thinking of Chevy Chase singing "Moon River" in *Fletch*.) He seemed to enjoy his work.

After he was done ripping my flesh off, he piled huge quantities of soap suds high over me and scrubbed some more. Let's just say that it stung.

A lot.

Then he vigorously shampooed my head—*and face*—with his massive hands while squatting like a bare-chested catcher in a miniskirt directly front of me. (Great visual burned into my memory, thanks.) He finally dumped dozens of gallons over my head, effectively water-boarding me there on the marble slab in my school girl outfit with bucket after bucket of painfully hot then bone chillingly cold water. The lawyer in me kept thinking that there was likely a cogent legal argument that this practice falls squarely within the definition of "torture," even under the Bush administration. (Too much? Sorry.)

I was sent to the reception area and ordered to change into a new skirt. I considered making a run for it but the truth is that I was heavily sedated from all the heat and the scrubbing and the soaping and the water and was frankly a bit docile from all the mental and physical abuse. So I changed and obediently waited in the reception area.

I sat quietly in one corner of the room. (*Maybe they will forget about me.*) After a few moments, I saw a second large Turk in a skirt approach in my periphery. I cowered in my school girl outfit. He reached out for me and helped me to my feet. Like the others who had come before him, he spoke little English but it didn't matter. I tuned him out completely after he uttered two simple words that I understood all too well.

"Oil massage."

That's right, I had a twenty minute baby oil rub down from a man twice my size in a filthy little Turkish bathhouse behind a metro station in Istanbul. And this was not the type of massage where you lay face down the whole time. No no, friends, it was not nearly so easy. I was forced to sit up and face my topless attacker repeatedly as he energetically oiled me from head to toe. (Again, thanks for the memories.)

I dressed and left in a hurry, but not before I was met at the door by both men, who "reminded me" to tip them. I forked over twenty lira more and broke through the doors into the fresh air and bright sunlight outside the *hamam*.

Freedom never felt so sweet.

Not surprisingly, my experience at the bath house left me a bit jumpy and perhaps more stressed and tense than I had been before it all started. I needed something, anything, to calm down.

I needed *tobacco*. A massive quantity of tobacco. And luckily for me, there is perhaps no better way to deliver an anesthetizing dose of that magical narcotic than the Turkish *nargile*, which is effectively a large water pipe used to smoke flavored tobacco leaves.

Maybe I should qualify this. For the record, I am not a

smoker and generally like to keep at least somewhat fit. With that said, I occasionally—very occasionally—like to remind myself of all the reasons I don't enjoy tobacco. And I had never tried one of these hookah-like contraptions. And everybody was doing it all around us. And they all seemed to be enjoying it.

And I am a total and complete sucker for this kind of thing.

After I recounted my *hamam* experience to Wendi in painstaking detail, we grabbed the kids and scrambled to a little restaurant/bar on a very cool street near our apartment where we had hung out and had dinner a few times. We got the girls going on this new kids' version of backgammon they learned (all the coffee shops and restaurants and bars have backgammon boards in Istanbul and lots of people play so the girls were eager to learn) and had a drink.

Then I ordered up a *nargile* stuffed full with apple and mint flavored tobaccos. (Yum.)

The tobacco is literally soaked for days in whatever fruit or herb or spice you can think of. Then it is packed into the *nargile* and lit by red-hot hot coals. You are given a little personalized mouthpiece to ensure cleanliness.

All you have to do is inhale.

The smoke from the tobacco is forced through some water down at the bottom of the *nargile* so that it is cooled significantly and does not sear your throat or lungs. I was repeatedly told that there is no healthier way to smoke tobacco. (An oxymoron, yes, but one that helps assuage the reluctant *nargile* user.) It is surprisingly smooth and flavorful, and it is something that was worth doing, even if only once. I stayed (mostly) out of the girls' field of vision and must say that I generally enjoyed the experience. I was teased a few times for not smoking it right and then again for not finishing it off, but I did re-achieve a state of relaxation and our whole gang went to bed happy for a restful night of sleep.

The fact is that Istanbul is a wonderful city that is literally filled with fantastic things to do for adults (including amongst many other things both Turkish baths—yes, I actually enjoyed the *hamam*—and *nargiles*). I must admit, however, that after my day doing a few of those things, I was happy to go back to playing Uno and Trouble and chess and backgammon in parks with Lily and Kate.

After all is said and done, maybe some of the coolest things we get to do as adults is play with our kids. (And use obscene quantities of tobacco after long days at the spa, when they aren't looking, naturally.)

CHAPTER 22
UNDER AFRICAN SKIES

Franschhoek, South Africa
October 2011

Take all of your money, give it all to chari-dee-dee-dee-dee.
—Bradley Nowell (Sublime)

---

*I*N THE PAST NEARLY FOUR MONTHS, *my wife and I have spent long evenings after the kids were asleep in secluded farmhouses deep in the green fields and gorgeous surroundings of the Irish and Italian countrysides. We've wandered the streets of the City of Light and the Eternal City. We've watched the sunset from a barge drifting on the rivers and canals of central France and from the beaches of the Etruscan coast. We've explored walled Tuscan cities and laid side-by-side on an idyllic Croatian island. We've stood hand-in-hand in awe of the Blue Mosque and Aya Sofia at dusk.*

It is thus ironic that the most romantic moment of the entire trip came a few nights ago in a rooftop Airstream trailer park in Cape Town, South Africa.

That was the beginning of the blog I sat down to write a couple days ago. That is the blog I *should* be writing right now.

But I can't.

I *should* be telling you that we took a wonderful flight from Istanbul to Dubai for an overnight layover (fly Emirates if you haven't, it is a totally different and fantastic flying experience that really caters to kids and adults alike) and then made the long (but still pleasant; I'm telling you, fly Emirates) nine-hour flight from Dubai to Cape Town.

And I *should* be spending the next couple thousand words (roughly) telling you that we truly loved Cape Town and the well-appointed trailer park we stayed in above *The Grand Daddy Hotel* for four nights. I should be regaling you with stories of the beauty of *Kirstenbosch National Botanical Garden* and the evening "aerial cableway" (read "gondola") ride we took up the side of *Table Mountain*. I should be telling you how much we all loved an afternoon at *World of Birds Wildlife Sanctuary and Monkey Park*, and of how the harbor at *Haut Bay* reminded us—a little bit, anyway—of the Santa Barbara Waterfront and home. I should be skimming a thesaurus right now on a hunt for superlatives to adequately convey the beauty of the beaches and the African Penguins at *The Boulders*. I should be recounting our delicious meals and repeated discussions of how the beach communities around *Sea Point* are reminiscent of early versions of many now-thriving and exclusive southern California beach enclaves. I should be telling you that we have found Cape Town and environs a surprisingly comfortable place, one that we could see living and raising a family in, maybe—even despite some obvious political, economic and social issues and scars (or still-open wounds) from all too recently righted wrongs.

I *should* be writing all of that. Every bit of it is true.

But, like I said, I can't. I just can't seem to focus on all that now that we have arrived at *Bridges of Hope* in Franschhoek and spent the past few days with seventy-five African kids from a number of "townships" from surrounding areas.

("Townships" is in quotes because I believe it is a misleading term. These "townships" are no more "towns" than a homeless camp rigged with electricity is a "city." From the outside, living conditions appear at best deplorable, and it is difficult to think of how many people are forced to live in them in a country that otherwise seems to be headed in the right direction and doing pretty well from a socio-economic perspective.)

Before I get started, it is worth saying that it is not my intention to be too heavy here. This is indeed a family trip and we are doing our best to keep it light and entertaining and fun. But being here at *Bridges* and having this experience is not particularly easy, and it is difficult to find much humor in it. The truth is that this has already been one of the most—if not the most—difficult and rewarding and eye-opening experiences we have had to date. It just isn't particularly funny or light.

Bridges is a Santa Barbara-based non-profit that we came across many months ago as we looked at potentially coming to South Africa and doing some volunteer work. We met with (delightful) founders Dennis and Susan Wadley at their church in Goleta, and learned that they had a vision years ago of doing something to help kids in South Africa (and later in Ethiopia) who some might accurately describe as "extremely disadvantaged" or "lacking any meaningful opportunities." After just a few days here, I personally would describe them as kids that the world has let fall through the cracks in many ways, and who are forced to endure a full lifetime of indescribable hardship that you and I cannot imagine. Whatever terms you use, however, Dennis and Susan and their skilled team—including, by the way, a few UCSB students who are here and helping out for the week (go Gauchos!)—have created an oasis where these particular kids get a chance to spend a few days actually acting like kids in a comfortable and supportive environment, just as your kids and mine do every day.

The reality is that *Bridges* is making a meaningful, tangible difference in people's lives, every day. It is an inspired and inspiring place, and we are lucky to be able to spend a week here participating in two separate three-day camps. The first group of kids showed up a few days ago and just left yesterday.

What an experience it has been so far.

We have all heard lots of stories of "amazing kids" living in extreme poverty and dire conditions. And that is certainly one way to characterize the group of kids we met and played with for the past few days. But the most difficult personal realization for me—and I don't mean this in any derogatory way—was that these kids are no more "amazing" than any other kids. They are just kids, like yours and mine. They love attention and affection and games and they cry and they fight and they misbehave.

But these kids come from homes that have been broken and re-broken and broken again, and they have seen and lived through things that most of us (thankfully) cannot imagine. Basic needs that we take for granted—food, shelter, healthcare, education—are sometimes (or often) unmet. You can see it in their actions and in their behavior. Sometimes you can see it in their faces.

And they are just kids, like yours and mine.

It's heartbreaking. There is no more appropriate word to describe it. Frankly, it can be difficult to "enjoy" being here, especially when you stop and consider the harsh realities.

Fortunately, the kids themselves actually make enjoying this time pretty easy. They are, um, let's see, *rationally* exuberant (take that, Alan Greenspan) and excited and enthusiastic about being here. And with a trampoline, swimming pool, loaded game room, soccer field and basketball court (amongst other fun stuff), what kid wouldn't be?

The place is like a powder keg that could at any moment

erupt into total chaos marked by laughter and yelling and general frolicking (yes, frolicking). Although many of these kids have been hardened by their experiences, simply acknowledging them and talking to them eventually draws huge smiles. Lily and Kate are tremendously popular and quickly and easily break down barriers that may have otherwise stood between us. Wendi's patience and charming smile and ease with kids make everything flow very naturally. And after some getting to know each other on the soccer field, I taught about twenty kids how to run the "high-five-snap-knuckle-bump" and they were floored, laughing hysterically. Then I fell into my role as a human jungle-gym, which suits me just fine.

The kids really like to touch all of us—especially our hair and hands—and learn how old we are and our names and basic stuff about where and how we live. (Some haven't ever heard of the United States or California.) We are happy to oblige.

We spent a bunch of time looking after one little boy ("Sino," short for Sinoyolo) since he is not part of the camps but instead the brother of one of the counselors, and had him into our little apartment to play games or have a snack or to watch a movie on the laptop. (It is overwhelmingly likely that you have never heard more sounds of amazement and enjoyment in response to the movie *Tangled* or a game of Uno.) He sort of became a member of our little group and was a great friend to both girls and us, always laughing and joking and eager to help out.

We spent our first night playing with everybody and watching old Warner Bros. cartoons (hilarious, by the way ... where did they go?) and a slideshow of photographs of the kids' first day here.

It is hard to describe the happy anarchy that came when the first pictures appeared on the screen. Kate and Lily and I sat amongst a dozen or so kids who were literally all over me and basically petting my daughters as they alternatively stared, mouths gaping, at the screen and then erupted into fits of laughter and playful wrestling. At one point, Kate reached out and touched a little boy's head and hair and looked up at me with a smile and said, "Soft, daddy."

When we got back to the apartment, Lily asked me why the kids had been climbing and laying and sitting all over me and yelling and touching and asking all about us. I told her, as gently as possible, stammering and stumbling and mumbling, that these kids are a bit different than many other kids she knows for lots of reasons.

"Yeah," she said, "like they roughhouse a lot more."

Believe it or not, that seemingly innocuous statement scared me. The fact is that neither Lily nor Kate has ever once said anything about the color of these kids' (or anyone else's) skin or about the clothes they wear or the way they talk or look. And while it was clear that Kate was interested in the little boy she touched during the slideshow, it is clear to me that she was just that: Interested. The recognition of all the purported "differences" people see—and the translation of those differences into more negative divisions—is clearly something taught to and learned by our kids.

They sure ain't born with it.

The *scary* thing for me was the realization, in that moment, that Wendi and I, as parents, have the responsibility for ensuring that our kids do not learn those types of lessons. To the best of my recollection, that particular issue never came up in *What to Expect When You're Expecting* or the Dr. Spock book.

We have a small apartment here with a kitchen but are eating as many meals with the kids as possible. (That is the point of being here, after all.) Lunch yesterday was four slices of bread with shredded bologna and cheese with an orange. This seemed to be a huge deal and both Lily and I at one table and Wendi and Kate at another across the room ate little and shared most. Lily and I watched the kids devour every last crumb on their plates. Then we saw one of our table mates effectively eat an orange rind.

Nobody likes eating orange rinds.

That really got me thinking about the day-to-day living conditions these kids endure. The mentality that they have developed as a function of those living conditions speaks volumes about their experience and view of the world: *I'd better eat as much as possible right now, in this meal, because I can't be sure when my next meal might be.* And this remains the case here at *Bridges*, where there is plenty of food for everyone and the kids are well-fed. It is a sobering thought.

Dinner was chicken with rice and sweet potatoes and cole slaw. Lily and I finished as much of our dinners as we could and then gave our slaw and potatoes away. When I stood up to bring our dishes to the kitchen, one of the girls at our table picked through the food that remained on our plates and took both of our chicken wings—which we thought we had finished and were ready for the trash bin—and gobbled them down.

It was a powerful moment that I will never forget. It broke my heart and infuriated me all at once. It made me want to grab my kids and never let them go. It made me want to do something, anything, to help balance the brutal inequities of the world that were quite literally staring me in the face. I felt powerless watching that little girl, stunned by the depth and enormity of the social, moral and ethical problem I was witnessing first hand; but at the same time I felt more empowered to do the right thing and make a difference than I've ever felt.

It turned out that Wendi, who had again been sitting across the room with Kate, had a very similar experience. And as we sat up talking about what had happened that night and the events of the previous few days, it became very clear that Lily and Kate are not the only ones learning and experiencing new and meaningful things as we travel. Wendi and I, alongside our two daughters, are seeing things together that will impact each of us and all of us for the rest of our lives.

And we are only just starting to scratch the surface.

So, you ask, what about that romantic evening in a Cape Town trailer park that I *should* have been writing about? In addition to the mock introduction set forth many words above, I had roughed up a conclusion, which follows, unchanged from the first draft. And although it predates our time at *Bridges*, I actually think it is an appropriate end, even now, and that it remains relevant to the experiences of the past few days. Judge for yourself.

Wendi and I stayed up late after the kids went to sleep in the trailer and drank too many watermelon martinis (her) and rum and cokes (me) and talked about our favorite apartments and houses and dinners and times together over the past sixteen years. We talked of our trip and of the places we've been and the people we've met and the experiences we've shared.

And we discussed all the things we've learned about ourselves and our daughters and our family since we left. And we agreed that we were glad to be there, in a trailer park high above Cape Town, together, with our kids, as a family.

And we laughed like old friends for hours.

Under a beautiful African night sky.

CHAPTER 23
SURF SAFARI

Addo Elephant National Park, South Africa
October 2011

All I need are some tasty waves, a cool buzz and I'm fine.
—Jeff Spicoli

I RODE MY FIRST WAVE when I was fifteen years old. My family lived forty-five minutes from the Bodega Coast in northern California but I started hanging around with a couple older guys from my high school who had surfed for years with their fathers and older brothers and eventually hitched a ride. I took an absolute pounding for the first month or so but I persevered and eventually got the hang of it and began thinking of myself as a "surfer."

Surfing at *Salmon Creek* or *Goat Rock* or *Portuguese Beach* in the early 1990s was not like surfing in Santa Barbara today. There were relatively few guys back then, and they formed a small surfing community. You'd see the same dozen regulars through the fog in the parking lots or paddling out. Everybody would hoot and holler for good waves, and there was a fair amount of sharing and a lot of camaraderie. Some guys might even offer a gallon milk container or mid-sized cooler filled with hot water over a conversation after a session in the frigid waters. (It was so damn cold out there that the most important feature I looked for in my first car was a powerful floor heater. A rusted out brown circa-1980 Subaru wagon did the trick nicely.) I fell in love with the whole scene right away, even despite the bitter cold and skittish and unpredictable weather and steep learning curve associated with fast, heavy waves in often difficult conditions.

I think what I liked most about surfing was that it was primarily a solitary endeavor. It provided time away from everything else and drew your focus in tight. I'd sit out there until my hands and feet could no longer function properly due to the cold and think and consider and reflect and surf. It was a far cry from the team sports I was brought up on (soccer, baseball, basketball, etc.), and I remember feeling like I had found something for me, and I didn't want to share it.

It's funny to look back through the lens of hindsight. The truth is that one could easily argue that surfing shaped my life in large part. I moved to Santa Barbara for what I then thought were warm waters and playful waves. (But now, seventeen years later, the water doesn't seem quite so warm and the waves don't seem quite so playful.) I attended UCSB because I loved the beach community and parties and people in Isla Vista, where I eventually met my wife. (She loved it too.) We lived in Summerland for a few years and grew to love Santa Barbara and environs and think of the area as a home, despite the fact that we both grew up in the Bay Area. We left only for me to attend law school and "start our real lives" back in San Francisco and Marin and after six or seven years and one child (with another on the way), we knew it was time to get back to the place we always called home.

We've been happy in Santa Barbara ever since.

For better or worse, I've surfed very little over the past

four or five (or six) years. Kids and a career and life basically happened, and I was not particularly good at carving out time for myself that way. The truth is that I got so far from it that I forgot how much I missed the ritual of taking a drive along the coast by myself or with a friend, finding the spot, waxing the stick up, strapping on the wetsuit, paddling out and taking an hour or two (or three) away from everything, like I had done so many times throughout my youth.

That all changed this week.

We spent our last few days around *Bridges of Hope* staying involved in the camps and enjoying our time. The kids and staff and volunteers were really wonderful and embraced us and made us feel welcome and at home. I was even given the opportunity to visit *Philippi*, one of the "townships" referred to in my last post in which at least some of the kids attending the camps live, and I jumped at it. Wendi and the girls stayed back, mostly as a safety precaution after we were told, in no uncertain terms, that this was not always the friendliest place to visit and that the kids may call too much attention our way.

I drove the cherry red *Hyundai Atos Prime* we rented a couple weeks ago (what, you've never heard of an *Atos Prime*?) nearly an hour back toward Cape Town with my guide, a twenty-year old woman from *Bridges* who lives in the area and knows some of the kids. She talked of her life and the conditions of her upbringing and the challenges she faces as a poor black South African woman going forward. That is a difficult conversation to have, sort of, when you live in a place like Santa Barbara and have a world of opportunity at your finger tips. But it is reality here (and many other places, both foreign and domestic), and seeing it and hearing it from the perspective of the truly disadvantaged is as bleak and void and sad as you might think.

Philippi is much as I thought it would be, unfortunately, overcrowded and marked by poor living conditions and shack after shack constructed of every conceivable building material or scraps of whatever happened to be available, with dirt floors, little or no plumbing, shared bathrooms, inadequate or nonexistent waste removal, etc. I was taken to a church with a soup kitchen and hung out for a half-hour or so, talking to some locals and taking pictures and showing them to everybody on the screen on my camera to huge laughs. It was fun because the people made it fun, but evidence of extraordinary challenges—hunger, disease, lack of housing—was all around me.

It seemed to be going well, so my guide agreed to take me to a nearby "informal settlement," which is effectively an officially recognized homeless camp. *Sweet Home*—sarcasm or irony, you decide—was made up of a series of dirt roads with deep potholes and trash strewn about, shacks cobbled together out of garbage, no electricity or plumbing, animals and sewage and who knows what else all over the place, people living and raising their families in truly heartbreaking conditions.

I was taken to a day care for young kids, maybe 2-4 years old, and they went wild for a visitor with a camera. I was literally overrun by toddlers; they were grabbing and crying and holding on to my legs and arms and hair and ears. I actually thought that the camera wasn't going to make it at one point. But eventually I started snapping shots of whatever happened to be in front of the lens and then playing the shots back for the kids. They calmed a bit and then went nuts for the slideshow.

After another half-hour or so, it was time for us to go so that the kids could take a nap. (The thought of getting all those kids down after I had riled them all up made me laugh, privately.) I asked to stay a bit longer, perhaps, and see a few more things so I could try to take some pictures but was told that it was getting later and that this was a bad idea. It turns out that white foreigners driving around in bright red rental cars with expensive cameras don't always fare so well in *Philippi* and *Sweet Home*.

We headed back to Bridges and barely spoke a word. I was truly lost in my own world of thought, and I think my guide was too. For me, seeing *Philippi* and *Sweet Home* firsthand was a bit difficult to understand and process; and for her, showing *Philippi* and *Sweet Home* to me was probably the same.

We finished the week out with a big bonfire and talent show, which was a treat for all of us. There was African song and dance and music and short plays and a lot of fun, even though we couldn't understand a word of most of it. The kids (and many of the counselors) primarily spoke *Xhosa*, which is probably as foreign a language as you can imagine, complete with a variety of clicks and other sounds that have no home in the Roman alphabet. We stayed up well into the night laughing and talking and joining in the songs and having a blast.

It was a challenging week but a good one that none of us will forget. Much (or all) of what is happening there at *Bridges* has a foundation in Christianity, and religion and religious doctrine is openly utilized as a tool for teaching morals and values. It may come as no surprise to many of you that organized religion has never really been a big part of my life, and I have my reasons for that, but I must admit that I witnessed and gained a true appreciation for a different side of the church that I knew about and recognized but hadn't actually seen with my own eyes before. It was inspiring and practical and tolerant and considerate. And it provided something important that many of these kids did not have before they stepped off the bus that delivered them to *Bridges*.

It provided hope.

You could see that in the kids' faces just as sure as you could see the desperation in their faces, sometimes, when they sat down and talked to you. And I learned that ultimately it doesn't matter to me whether that hope comes from organized religion or corporate money or mysticism or whatever. I'm just glad that *Bridges* is there and that it is effective at accomplishing its mission. We were privileged to have the experience we did.

Bridges also had an unexpected side-effect. After finishing out our week there, I truly craved some time in the water to decompress a bit. And we had four free days before our reservation at the *Addo Elephant National Park* was to start. So I ran to a local shop and bought a used board and a leash.

And I went surfing.

The truth is that we had always planned to drive the south coast of Africa after *Bridges* and before the *Addo*. The *Garden Route* is a five or six hour drive that basically takes you along the water from *Mossel Bay*, a small beach community, to *Jeffrey's Bay*, a globally known surf destination that at least some would argue is the best right point in the world. There are loads of small bays and towns and beautiful forests and wilderness along the way, and we planned to take a few days to explore (and surf) it.

(Oh, I almost forgot. Before we left Franschhoek, which not only happens to be *Bridges'* address but also the center of a famous South African wine region, we had a great time at *Spier Winery* near Stellenbosch. Slight over-consumption of the *21 Gables Chenin Blanc* before and during a long lunch in a tree fort led to a "Cheetah Encounter" that, looking back, could have easily resulted in the fatal mauling of one of our children. Sorry for the interruption.)

We didn't get very far on the *Garden Route*. *Mossel Bay* is a cool little town reminiscent of Santa Cruz(ish) with a few consistently decent to good waves. I surfed *Outer Bowls* at *The Point* a couple times—the water is cool but trunks and a long sleeve wetsuit top work just fine for an hour or maybe two—and had a blast reacquainting myself with surfing. Wendi and the kids hung out on the beach or did some homeschool or went to the local Farmers Market.

After a couple days, we drove another forty-five minutes east to *Vic Bay*, which is really nothing more than a little tropical canyon into the Indian Ocean with a few houses on it and a beach. It also happens to have a fun little right point. We lucked out and found a reasonable family-sized room right on the water about mid-wave, where we could sit on our balcony and watch the surf and the beach action and I could run down whenever "the crowd"—never once more than 10 guys, and that was on a busy Sunday—thinned out. The surf was double-overhead and a bit sloppy with light onshore winds the first day but then the conditions cleaned up and the place fired. I even started to work out my surfing situation for the first time in years, which was gratifying (relieving?). And my wife and kids watched me do it and hooted and hollered from the balcony, just like I was back in Bodega again. It was a perfect re-introduction to surfing and we all loved it (maybe especially me).

But there was a problem. We ran out of time too fast in *Vic Bay* and had to get to our reservation at the *Addo*.

That was when all hell broke loose.

We were all so zenned out from a few days of nothing but beaches and waves and home cooked meals and evening glasses of wine and/or beer that we basically forgot many of the travel skills and rules we've learned over the past four months. And we did something stupid, frankly, that put all of us in danger.

Instead of getting exact driving directions from *Vic Bay* to the *Addo*, we relied solely on the instructions provided by our iPad. The iPad is a truly indispensible travel tool and it can be used to innumerable good and beneficial ends, one of which is accurate and reliable directions anywhere in the world. It has literally never led us the wrong way (although we think it provided a longer drive once or twice in Italy where it could have selected an alternative and perhaps shorter route, but no harm, no foul). With that said, we have always input a precise destination, an address or hotel near where we were headed, to be sure that there were no mistakes. And we would typically quickly double check the directions against a paper map to be sure that they made sense.

We did none of that for our drive to the *Addo*.

We hadn't had an internet connection for a couple days in *Vic Bay*, which is actually pretty isolated. When we finally found the sole spot in the bay that would allow us to get online via a terrible (pirated) connection bummed off of a reluctant local, we hastily typed in *"Addo Elephant National Park"* as our destination and took off as soon as the directions came up.

We took none of the precautions we would normally take, and we paid for it.

The truth is that it was a big mistake, one that we never should have made. We input a very general location—a huge game park composed of hundreds of square miles in the middle of South Africa. We didn't know it but the iPad had simply given us directions to the geographic middle of the park without regard for entry gates or the actual position of our "double chalet with a game viewing terrace."

A colloquialism comes to mind: "[Bleep] in, [bleep] out."

What should have been a pretty simple four hour drive in the *Atos Prime* over good (read "paved") roads through safe portions of South Africa turned into a ten-plus hour drive over terrible dirt roads through the less frequented portions of the country far from anything on the typical tourist map. When we finally realized how lost we were, the sun was low in the sky and the gas gauge was reading (very) near empty.

Being lost in this particular part of South Africa is not at all like being lost in California. We were literally in the middle of nowhere, no cars or people or houses or hotels or villages anywhere, no gas stations for sometimes hundreds of kilometers, baboons and hyenas and monkeys all over the roads and the warnings of many South African natives to not drive at night in the bright red rental car with the kids ringing loudly in both my ears and Wendi's.

As circumstances developed, we soon realized that we were in a very bad place. And we were very far from anywhere we wanted to be.

Stress started giving way to fear that we would actually (seriously) be forced to sleep in our car with our kids and all of our stuff (including, by the way, a guitar and surfboard, which were further cramping the small cockpit of the *Atos Prime*) somewhere in the middle of nowhere in Africa.

These are the moments when you wonder how in the hell you are in the middle of some country in Africa in a rented POS on empty with your young daughters at dusk rather than in your comfortable home in Santa Barbara. It is also the type of situation that really tests a family's ability to withstand the stress of extended travel. I must say that Wendi stayed impeccably calm in the face of a terrible situation and really mellowed the whole family out. I was starting to get pretty, ah, *tense*, and she completely kept her cool. We literally stopped the car, stayed calm, rationally discussed what was happening and made a good decision at the last possible moment. There was no fighting, no finger pointing and no whining or crying. The kids were quiet and well-behaved, and I think they very clearly understood what was happening. We worked together as a team.

And we figured it out.

When we did that, good fortune smiled upon us. A local hunter magically appeared out of nowhere on a four-wheeler and I flagged him down. When I told him where we were headed, he looked puzzled and then laughed right in my face. We were about a hundred miles in the wrong direction, with nothing of any consequence around us. The only gas within hundreds of kilometers was in a small town, he said, fifty or sixty kilometers from where we stood. He pointed us in the right direction and we trusted him. We eventually found the gas station, with the needle firmly pinned to the peg below empty. I'm not sure how close we were to running out of gas, but it was close. Really close.

We carefully consulted the iPad—which was down to only five percent of its battery life—and figured out where we needed to go (again based on the hunter's comments) and decided to make a run for it. (Sort of the lesser of two evils since staying in the remote town with the gas station was not an appealing option, trust me.) We drove through sunset and had found some well-traveled highways by the time night rolled around.

We finally pulled into the *Addo* around 8:30 p.m., more than ten hours after we'd started.

If we had gone the right way we were looking at around a three or four hour drive. I couldn't tell you what roads we traveled if I had a map in front of me, and I sincerely doubt that the town with the small gas station would be on it anyway. It was no fun for any of us, and it will not happen again. (For the record, we have driven in every country we've visited, except Turkey, without major mishap.)

It didn't end there, either. When we woke up the next morning to do our first drive of the game park, one of the tires on the *Atos Prime* was flat. (Another colloquialism: "When it rains, it pours.") I have no idea if we had been driving around on it the night before but it wouldn't surprise me. I was so focused on getting my wife and kids to a safe place that it could have easily gone unnoticed. And stopping to change it would not have been a good thing, so maybe it is better that I missed it (if I did).

I changed the tire (there is no triple-A out here) much to the amusement of my wife and we took off for a drive around the *Addo*. It was great; I don't know if we were lucky or what but we were treated to a wide variety of beasts in large numbers. Some people see nothing at these game parks since you simply drive around their vast terrain trying to spot one or more of the "Big Five" or the "Big Seven" or the "Big Three," depending upon where you are.

We were thrilled to find a herd of massive African Elephants (world's largest land animals!) walking in line no more than thirty feet from the *Atos Prime* to a watering hole, and were the only people on it for ten minutes. We've also seen zebras and kudu and Cape buffalo and warthogs and eland and tons of other creatures (including the endemic African Dung Beetle, which drew roars of laughter from Lily and Kate, and thus from me, at each sighting) just feet from the car.

Lily was initially horrified by the big animals—she likes the "mid-sized" animals, she says—but has mellowed due primarily to Kate's gentle words reassuring her, for example, that the absolutely huge bull elephant right beside us "couldn't get us in the car, so don't worry." (Oh, to be four again.) We are having fun, more fun than I personally thought we'd have here.

But we had a close call. Too close.

You know what they say, though, and there is indeed a (bright, shiny) silver lining behind the cloud that we lived under for a few hours. It has me craving a surf again.

And J-Bay is only an hour away.

We just put off our flight to India for an extra week to be sure we have enough time to find it.

CHAPTER 24
KARMIC (IN)JUSTICE

Cape Town, South Africa
October 2011

Karma karma karma karma karma chameleon.
—Boy George (*Culture Club*)

SOUTH AFRICA HAS BEEN A GOOD MANY THINGS to us. It's been easy and hard and beautiful and ugly and hot and cold and heavy and light and, well, you get the idea. Lots of thought-provoking contrast and, frankly, quite a bit of fun for all ages. From the funky hip scene in and around Cape Town to the vast vineyards of Stellenbosch and Franschhoek to the untouched beaches and the majestic mountains of the *Garden Route*. From the rewarding volunteer work and time spent playing with new friends to the rejuvenating surfing and simplicity of relaxing without much else to do. From the (wild) animals of the *Addo Elephant National Park* to the (party) animals of *Jeffreys Bay*. It's all been great, and we've really enjoyed the past month here.

Perhaps best of all, however, is that we accidentally achieved at least some degree of enlightenment. We inadvertently stumbled across an answer to one of the world's great mysteries. We—the Mazzas from Santa Barbara—actually discovered a universal truth that is absolutely undeniable.

It's karma, man. And it's far out.

After recovering from the driving and flat tire debacle described in *Surf Safari* and spending a few delightful days at the *Addo Elephant National Park*, we jumped back into the *Atos Prime* for a short drive to *Jeffreys Bay*. Although none of us said it, I think we were all feeling the same way. A bit tired, and ready to relax—especially right before heading to India, which we expect to be a relatively challenging (but very exciting!) portion of our trip. All of us were thus very happy, relieved even, when we pulled into *J-Bay*.

J-Bay is the quintessential surf town of years past. It is the kind of place where a little respect goes a long way, and we found the locals to be nothing but friendly and welcoming, even in the water. There is a very (even extremely) laid back attitude and ambiance. We visited out of the high season, so the town was slow and we saw few tourists in its shops and restaurants. We had no problem quickly finding a little hippie beach shack called *Dreamland* that just happens to be right on *Supertubes*—the highlight wave amongst many good or great ones scattered throughout the area's myriad coves and points and bays and endless beaches. We met owners and proprietors Thomas Petersen and his wife Jose, and moved right in.

Dreamland was a great place for us, perfect, even. Not only is there a world-class wave right out the front door, but the powdery beaches are also uncrowded and beautiful, teaming with great shells and tide pools and room to run and play. There is not much else to do—except for a fun beachside pee-wee golf course and eating and drinking or maybe a movie—so we found plenty of time for creative homeschool ideas and reading and writing and playing guitar and singing and dancing and otherwise enjoying our situation.

Thomas and Jose have been here for over fifteen years and are really knowledgeable about all things *J-Bay*. They were great friends and neighbors—Jose even cooked us the most delicious vegetarian meal we've ever had—and our stay at their place was just what the proverbial doctor ordered.

Thomas is super dialed into the surf scene and has tons of local and historical knowledge that he shares, and he even let me bum a wetsuit and then a board after I buckled the used one I bought back in Cape Town. (Yeah, I broke the surfboard I meant to sell before we left. But I'd started making a lot of waves and got greedy and busted it on one that I should have kicked out of but instead pulled into and got worked. These things happen in a place like this. It's a great wave with plenty of juice and speed.)

He and Jose have two sons. One is a quasi-pro surfer who is good enough to actually make it (he's just 18 and has made at least one video and won a few significant competitions, amongst other achievements with sponsors) and the other is an up and coming local grom. Surf or not, though, both boys are quick with a smile and made us feel really welcome.

After we put the girls down for bed, Wendi and I would sit on our deck and listen to the waves and the wind and play cards or guitar or whatever by candlelight and talk about nothing or everything. We'd look at the stars burning brightly against the contrast of an oily black night sea that can only really be seen in places far from the ambient light thrown off by boardwalks and beachside cities and freeways and mega-mansions. There were even a few thunder-and-lightening producing squalls that added to the whole scene.

Sleep came easy, deeply.

J-Bay is a happy place and was an easy one for us to be in. It is one of those spots in the world that is definitely worth hitting for anybody who can handle a funky little town with a serious wave and all the people and art and other good stuff that comes with those types of places. It's all there and we found it and fell quickly into it, like we have and will in other similar places.

We felt at home in *J-Bay*, and we certainly got the rest and relaxation we all craved. Fun times. Easy times. Smooth sailing in calm waters.

But there was a storm brewing during our stay in the *Dreamland* love shack. A ridge of high pressure marked by a fast approaching flight to India built and grew, and eventually collided with a low pressure system that had developed as a consequence of the fact that we had not yet obtained our Indian tourist visas.

In other words, we had purchased (fairly expensive) airline tickets to India but we couldn't actually get into India without first getting the visas we needed, and time was growing short. This started weighing on our minds, distracting us, harshing our *J-Bay* mellow. It eventually became a real issue that had the potential to wreak economic and travel havoc, and we were forced to deal with it.

This is an absurdly—even embarrassingly—long story, and I refuse to bore you with it. We had done our Indian visa research many weeks before all this actually went down, and I am confident that it was not completely our fault for lots of reasons. Let's just say that there was a misunderstanding. And after a few days of telephone calls and travel agents and visa services and general wheel-spinning in *J-Bay*, we made a decision. We jumped in the *Atos Prime* and drove eight hours straight back to Cape Town (rather than stopping in one or two more places along the *Garden Route* on our way), where we could sit down with the folks at the Indian embassy and the folks at Emirates and see what we could do without simply forfeiting thousands of dollars in airline tickets, which was looking increasingly likely from the view at *Dreamland*.

We arrived in Cape Town and checked back into *The Grand Daddy Hotel*, where we had spent five nights in a rooftop Airstream trailer when we first landed in South Africa. Then we spent two full days meeting and talking and planning and plotting. The Indian consulate was friendly and helpful but ultimately could not budge; they just can't issue visas in Cape Town, they said, only clear across the country in Durban or Johannesburg. (Two cities we long ago decided not to visit.) And the "recommended" solution of sending our passports—not copies but the actual passports themselves—clear across South Africa with some courier and endless paperwork and cash money was not a particularly comforting thought.

We ultimately decided that it was not worth the risk. Especially when we were told that it would take more than a week, maybe longer, to turn everything around, and that no visas were guaranteed for various reasons.

So we went to Emirates and met and talked and considered lots of alternatives, including (almost unthinkably) skipping Nepal and India—two longstanding and important places on our list of things we want to do—or heading to a beach in Sri Lanka for a couple weeks and hoping for the best with obtaining visas there. There were lots of complications (again, too boring to discuss), and we literally scoured world maps and guidebooks and airline hubs looking for the right solution.

Eventually, miraculously, a friendly Emirates airline representative helped us change our flight. I'm frankly not sure how it happened but, trust me, this was a big deal and we are thrilled. (Fly Emirates, I'm telling you.)

And we no longer have tickets to India.

Instead, we will be flying into *K-K-K-K-Kathmandu* (as Bob Seger would say). We had always planned on seeing Nepal (in fact, we had long ago arranged to do some additional volunteer work just outside Kathmandu), but had always thought we'd do it *after* India. In any event, we've adjusted our big picture plan a bit and should be able to obtain our Indian visas at the Indian embassy in Kathmandu without much problem and then head into Delhi and points south before flying out to southeast Asia.

In short, it's all good.

We are really excited to keep moving.

And so we find ourselves back in familiar Cape Town, staying at a great hotel on a street we know and love (although this time we are in a double room rather than an Airstream trailer on the roof). *The Grand Daddy* and its staff are fantastic and have been very accommodative to us throughout our time here. We are enjoying Cape Town even more than we did the first time we visited, and are glad for the second chance to wander the shops and cafes and the *Company's Garden* and the waterfront.

Yes, we are back to happy and stress-free times again and can't wait to land in Kathmandu. Looking back over the past few days, it is clear to us that we were lucky to work all of this out—it was a total nightmare, seriously—and that we may not have been so fortunate without the assistance of some good and beneficial force swirling around the universe.

We've spent the past four months purposefully and con-sciously doing our best to be good people throughout our travels. We smile at and are polite to everybody. We do our very best with local customs and languages. We tip well. We go out of our way to be friendly and spend time talking and answering questions. We don't haggle and bargain to the bitter end in an effort to save a dollar or two on the backs of the very people and places we visit. (We also are not suckers, of course.) We leave our hotel rooms and apartments clean.

I think it's fair to say that we are indeed good neighbors and world citizens (at least so far).

That's the whole point for us, really, we are quite intentionally spreading the love everywhere we go. Even under stormy skies and in choppy waters, we still do our very best to grin and remain calm and understanding and respectful. And we expect nothing in return for our (perhaps nauseating degree of) cheerfulness.

Nothing, perhaps, except a little karmic equity.

And now, with Kathmandu tickets in hand and the hang-ups and hold-ups of the Indian visa debacle behind us, we can confidently say that we understand karma. After all, we cashed ours in during our meeting with the Emirates representative, and we now know its cosmic value and truth firsthand.

We know that karma is *real*. In fact, we are living proof that particularly good karma can solve your most pressing problems.

Well, that's not exactly right.

We are living proof that particularly good karma—and around five hundred American dollars (it was a bargain, trust me)—will get you re-issued airline tickets to Kathmandu when all hope seems lost.

So keep taking the high road folks (and earning at least some money, just in case karma alone isn't enough to get you over the finish line). For what goes around, does indeed come back around to you.

Mostly, anyway.

CHAPTER 25
THE CURSE OF
THE TIBETAN HEALING BOWL

Kathmandu, Nepal
November 2011

I knew we should've bought that damn bowl.
—Wendi Mazza (yep, that's my wife)

---

*B*ONG.
I tried hard not to burst but a groundswell of uncontrollable laughter was quickly building inside me. I fought it with everything I had, not wanting to offend or anger the shopkeeper-*cum*-guru sitting in front of me, chanting softly.

"*Hold it together, Matthew,*" I pleaded with myself, "*you're a grown man for Christ's sake.*"

I sat cross-legged on the floor of a small shop high above Kathmandu near *Swayambhunath*, more commonly referred to (by us tourists, anyway) as the Monkey Temple. My eyes were closed but I could still see the shop's ancient walls and shelves lined with beautiful golden Nepali and Tibetan artifacts of all sorts of shapes and sizes, some brilliant and shiny and others dulled, subdued by the passage of time. Smoke coiled lazily to the ceiling from the incense burning on a small table in the far corner. Shafts of burnt yellow light cut cylinders through the stale air in the room.

I heard the sounds of a *sitar* somewhere in the distance.

I'd been lured into the shop fifteen minutes earlier by an old man. All outward appearances suggested only that he had a simple business peddling drinks to passersby. But after we'd sat and enjoyed our coffee shakes and apple *lassis*, he asked that I follow him to pay our bill. He nimbly led me down a narrow alley to a small, unassuming doorway, and I had to duck my head low to avoid banging it against the crooked and bent wood jamb under which he passed without thought.

And now there I sat, shoes off, with the red stain of his blessing marking my forehead, wearing a large Tibetan healing bowl turned upside-down on my head. He had struck the side of the bowl with a sizeable mallet, like a gong, causing it vibrate vigorously and emit a hypnotic din.

This man was no simple smoothie salesman.

The dam that was holding back my tidal wave of laughter was weakening. Fissures were developing. I began to panic.

Bong.

The instant the mallet made contact with the bowl for the second time, powerful vibrations began trickling down from the top of my head to my face and neck as raindrops find their way down a windowpane. First my eyes, then my ears and nose and mouth. Then my face and whole head. Then the vertebrae of my neck.

There was no more laughter. There was only feeling. A truly wonderful feeling.

"*There is really something to this bowl,*" I reconsidered. "*This is pretty cool.*"

Over time—I'm not sure how long—the vibrations found

their way into my chest and my belly. I slowly felt them develop in my arms and hands and fingers and fingertips. Then my hips and groin and legs and feet. Then my toes.

My whole body resonated like a tuning fork.

I could only barely make out the chanting and music. I visualized the ornate Buddhist inscriptions and carvings on the heavy golden bowl and saw again the somber look on the man's face when he described its healing and spiritual qualities. I smelled the incense. I breathed deeply.

Bong.

I saw myself and the shop and its keeper from above. I saw Wendi and Lily and Kate perusing the shops on the street outside, perhaps wondering where I had gone, perhaps not. There was no stress, no elation, no frustration. There only *was*.

My mind drifted to the past five days. The long flight from Cape Town to Dubai in the middle of the night. Kate sleeping on my lap and Lily sleeping on Wendi's in the airport as we read our novels and talked softly until morning and our flight to Kathmandu. The surreal taxi ride from the airport to our hotel. The suffocating sights and sounds and smells and tastes and feeling of the city.

I saw the potholed and broken streets crowded with people and animals and motorcycles and rickshaws and cars. I saw the goats and pigs and sheep butchered in open air and the litter strewn about everywhere and the myriad shops and filthy food stalls. I heard the dissonance of horns blasting from every imaginable mode of transportation and the indiscriminant yelling and the seemingly disordered mix of western and eastern music and babies crying. I smelled foreign spices and flavor combinations and incense and pollution. I tasted the gritty air. I saw the gangs of mischievous monkeys watching the passersby at *Swayambhunath*, waiting for an opportunity to swoop in and steal an apple or something shiny from tourists caught unawares.

I saw it all at once from a distance.

I witnessed the chaos that is Kathmandu.

Bong.

And then in an instant, it all changed. The chaos faded and was replaced by a feeling of warmth and understanding and peace with the very different world that had enveloped us for the past ninety-six hours.

I saw the people and children smiling and talking and laughing amongst what I previously saw as anarchy in its truest form, dancing with the cars and scooters and rickshaws as everybody worked together to make their way through clogged streets of dirt, mud and concrete. I saw the colorful dress and beautiful faces of the Nepali people and the kids playing amongst vibrant shops of all sorts (and even then some). I saw the temples of *Durbar Square* basking in their ancient beauty and glory, and the monkeys wandering the massive golden Buddha sculptures and shrines. I recalled climbing the hundreds of steep steps to *Swayambhunath*, one of the holiest Buddhist temples in Kathmandu, just as others have for many centuries.

I saw the vibrant fruits and vegetables sold on the streets and tasted the delicate *momos* (Nepali dumplings) and the curry and lentil soup and homemade yogurt and vegetables of *Daal Bhat Tarkari* and the balanced sweetness and spice of the ubiquitous tomato-based sauce that accompanies, in one form or another, nearly every meal. I saw the streets and alleys lined with candles and colorful offerings to the various deities—of the ox, of the dog—that are celebrated at part of the *Tihar* festival that we happened to time perfectly.

I heard the children singing songs to those same gods

on the streets, seeking money or food from the passersby in exchange for their playful melodies.

And I saw Wendi and Lily and Kate amongst it all, laughing by the glowing candlelight, as they went from shop to shop on the dusty streets of *Thamel* during the festival, discovering all sorts of new treasures and talking with proprietors about their wares and the significance of the candles and the designs and the songs.

I grasped that this place is inherently special, mystical even. The people are happy and warm. Most are quick to entertain and play with Lily and Kate, and seem to have a knack for eliciting smiles and laughter within a few seconds. The geography defies explanation (the famous peaks of the Himalayas are not far), especially when you consider what is surely a stark contrast between the mountains and the city life of Kathmandu.

I understood that amongst all the turmoil there is a simplicity here. Amongst the obvious challenges an ease. Amongst the pollution and the dirt and the dust a natural beauty.

Kathmandu is a special place indeed.

Bong.

Nothing. Nothing but comfort and peace and quiet in a place where those words are likely seldom used. No sight, no sound, no taste, no smell. No thoughts, no time.

No worries.

I heard a distant rattling. The rattle grew louder and louder until I could no longer ignore it. Something was calling me.

I opened my eyes.

The bowl was no longer on my head and I had no idea when it had come off. In fact, I truly had no idea how long I had been in the little shop. Could it have been...*hours?*

Wendi and the girls were now in the room and the shopkeeper was talking softly. He gently turned to Wendi and placed the bowl on her head. He spent the next however many minutes taking her through the same ritual I had experienced. I can't say how long it took because I remained in a trance-like state, still resonating with each strike of the bowl as it sat on my wife's head. The kids were mellowed, draped over me the whole time. We were all affected, and there was a distinct, undeniable change in all of our moods upon entering the shop and feeling the power of the bowl.

At some point, the shopkeeper removed the bowl from Wendi's head too, and I began to understand that he was telling us how to use the bowl for massage and steam baths and how it could heal us and provide relief from stress and anxiety and disease. It was a new heirloom, he said, one that would always remind us of Nepal, of this place and time, and that could be passed from generation to generation without noticeable blemish or any lessening of energy and power.

I looked across at Wendi and saw that she was nodding her head in agreement. I realized that I was nodding, too.

"The bowl is magical," I thought. *"We must have one. We must pass it down from Mazza to Mazza to Mazza. Yes, the bowl is magical."*

It was not a word that awakened Wendi and me from our semi-consciousness and brought us back to the real world.

It was a number.

"$375 American dollars," he was repeating, almost chanting, softly. "$375 American dollars."

Wendi looked at me as if to ask, "Are we really going to start wearing a Tibetan healing bowl on our heads in our living room in California?"

I was thinking the same thing.

I tucked my credit card back into my open wallet.

"Thanks, my friend," I said, "I appreciate your time but we cannot purchase the bowl."

"But it is your bowl," he said, "*it has chosen you*. Make me an offer."

So I did.

"*Namaste*," he said, "you will be back."

———•———

I think we've regretted not buying the bowl that day. It was unique and beautiful, and would have definitely reminded us of the Monkey Temple and the shop and Nepal every time we saw it. In many ways, the bowl *did* choose us. Each of us agreed that it had the best sound and vibrational qualities (every bowl is different and we easily reached consensus). And the whole experience in the shop was very cool and did indeed have a lasting effect on us.

With all that said, one of the (idealistic) points of our trip was to get away from the purely material world, a bit, anyway, and we have been buying entirely too much stuff and sending it home for later consumption or admiration or whatever. (In fact, we had literally just purchased prayer wheels and flags and clothes before sitting down for our smoothies.) So we declined on principle, sort of, consistent with the intentions that guided us to this point, mostly.

But there is a problem. In the days since we decided not to buy the bowl, Kate has spent a night vomiting from some stomach bug, and I have pulled a hamstring racing a few kids at *Mendies Haven* (a home for children outside of the city, more on it another time) and then a second whole day and night sleeping with an unexplained high fever and severe stomach bug. Even the previously impenetrable Wendi caught a nasty cold (thus prompting the opening quote).

Maybe the bowl chose us for a reason and could be healing

us all right now. Maybe this is its way of showing us that we need it. Maybe things will keep happening until we right the wrongs we have perpetrated.

Maybe the shopkeeper was right.

I knew we should've bought that damn bowl.

CHAPTER 26
THOUGHTS OF HOME

New Delhi, India
November 2011

In my mind, I'm going to [California].
Can't you see the sun shining?
Can't you just feel the moon shining?
Ain't it just like a friend of mine, to hit me from behind?
Yes, I'm going to [California] in my mind.
—James Taylor (adapted)

IT WAS BOUND TO HAPPEN eventually, I suppose.

We've thought of and talked about home and family and friends throughout our trip but the excitement and near constant anticipation of new places and experiences kept us from truly yearning for the things that we know, the things that comfort us most. The novelty, for lack of a better word, of extended travel had really sustained us and kept us quite happy and fulfilled for the past nearly five months.

Perhaps that novelty of constantly moving has worn a bit after all this time. Perhaps the lure of the familiar has grown because we are now in places that are so different in so many ways.

Or maybe we just miss the people and the place we call home.

It started innocently enough. I got a few emails related to my dormant (former?) law practice that required some thought and considered responses. That started a conversation between Wendi and I about what we might actually do, professionally and otherwise, when we return. That, in turn, started us talking about our old life in Santa Barbara, the one we loved (and still love), filled with the people and personalities and places that we know so well.

Then we talked about our coffee machine—it's a truly wonderful Italian contraption that spits out rich and wonderful espresso at the touch of a button—and our bed and our shower and our privacy and our dog and our friends and their kids and kindergarten and preschool and dinner parties and babysitters and adult time and too many drinks (occasionally) and laughing and talking (always).

We reminisced about long days and late evenings spent at Nun's and Butterfly and Summerland beaches and we gushed about San Francisco and Marin and Napa and Ojai and Los Olivos and California the good ole US of A and we talked about what we might do and eat when we get back and how it might feel and and and...

And we missed home, *truly* missed home, for the first time since we left.

——•——

Ok, so, where did I leave off?

Oh yes, the Tibetan healing bowl.

We did finally recover from the curse associated with our failure to purchase it. My fever subsided, Wendi's nose decongested and Kate stopped projectile vomiting all over our room. Lily somehow avoided affliction entirely. (We never did find another bowl we liked enough to buy and thus risk being haunted forever. If Kate begins the horrifying up-chucking again,

I will take a frickin' rickshaw from California or wherever we are to the Monkey Temple to put an end to it. Seriously.)

We spent the ensuing five days living at *Mendies Haven*, a home for orphaned children in a rural area outside of Kathmandu. The *Haven* has been run by the same family for around for fifty years, and has ties to Santa Barbara. (Two Westmont grads and a Brooks grad are among the generation that is now taking over the proverbial reins.) It provides a home in every sense of the word for around thirty Nepali children from as young as toddlers to as old as late teens or early twenties, whenever a given child is ready to support him or herself in the world outside the *Haven's* protective walls.

Education and religion and family are paramount. The children are loved, and the place feels very much like a big family rather than, say, an institution.

We lived in the girls' dormitory and did all the things you might imagine. Late night Chinese jump rope parties and hide-and-go-seek and friendship bracelets and Nepali games and Uno and slideshows of our house and friends etc. We ate meals with the kids but were also treated to all sorts of authentic, home-cooked Nepali dishes with Susan, Charles, Jessica and Daniel Mendies. We had long conversations over tea in Charles and Susan's modest living room that covered everything from Nepali culture and language to views on American politics and religion to war and everything in between. It was a real treat to hear educated, considered thought from those with an often far different (yet entirely reasonable) experience and perspective.

These are the things—food, conversation, understanding—that make travel fun and interesting. (We even learned to make a variety of delicious tea drinks from scratch, the Nepali way, which we will share when we get home, perhaps over a conversation in our own modest living room.)

Five days at *Mendies Haven* was physically, mentally and emotionally tiring, as you can imagine. Charles and Susan understood this and, without any prompting from us, arranged a room at a resort in the mountains high above the Kathmandu valley in *Nargakot*.

Wow. Generosity is an understatement.

It was a simple but extraordinary place. The air was clean and brisk and the mountains were green and lush and a misty fog materialized in the evening that only added to a feeling of sanctuary and serenity that may just be particular to south Asia. We relaxed and ate and drank (and the girls swam in the indoor pool and hot tub!) and slept soundly. We woke refreshed and were a bit disappointed to leave after only one night.

But Kathmandu beckoned. We needed to collect our Indian visas (yeah, still outstanding at that point, remember the Indian Visa Debacle?) and arrange for school shoes for the children at the *Haven* and do laundry and pay a few bills and send home an absurdly large box of "souvenirs" going back all the way to Istanbul. (So much for not buying too much stuff; this is the third or fourth box we've sent home.)

We got it all done and boarded a short flight bound for Delhi. (The flight plan took us north and then west along the *Annapurna* section of Himalayan range on a clear afternoon and we were treated to a few 25000 + foot peaks.) We'd been warned for months about the challenges associated with this particular city and India generally by friends and acquaintances and it seemed just about everybody we'd come across who has traveled there. We were prepared for what we believed would be the most difficult portion of our trip.

But, alas, things happen for a reason. There was indeed a reason we were forced into Nepal before India when things went awry with our Indian visas in South Africa. It turned out that Charles and Susan Mendies spent almost twenty years living and raising their children in Delhi, you see, and they offered to hook us up with a friend. That friend turned out to be Christel, a German scholar-turned-travel agent who has lived in India for nearly fifty years and knows Delhi about as well as any European might.

Christel got to work quickly, and really set us up.

She and our driver(!) collected us from the airport and took us to a very comfortable guest house-*cum*-apartment in *Greater Kailash I*, a fairly swanky south Delhi enclave. We got ourselves situated and had a good night's sleep in a city where that can be difficult given the congestion and noise. We awoke to a truly delightful Indian breakfast of thin potato pancakes filled with cauliflower and onion that we dipped in fresh yogurt and drizzled with a magical pickled-pepper oil and gobbled down with freshly brewed coffee. (The kids had eggs and toast and cereal and freshly squeezed orange juice.)

Then our driver and Christel took us sight-seeing around the city in a comfortable, air-conditioned car. We wandered the ancient ruins around *Qutub Minar* where Buddhists mixed with Hindus and Muslims; we sat in silence in the Baha'i House of Worship better known as the *Lotus Temple*; we lunched in a Hindu Temple dedicated to the sometimes mischievous *Krishna*; we got back to the apartment at a reasonable hour and were able to decompress—traveling around Delhi is indeed difficult and can feel a bit overwhelming, frankly, especially with two young blonde girls that attract more attention that we ever imagined possible—before heading out to dinner at one of a few nearby restaurants.

And then we did it again the next day. And the next.

We roamed the *Masjid-i Jahān-Numā* and then rickshawed through narrow alleys and ancient streets and markets of old Delhi; we grubbed at a jam-packed Delhi "canteen," where meals are simple and cheap and the tables are auctioned off to the higher bidders; we were blessed with coconuts and marigolds at a magnificent Hindu Temple focused on the powerful goddess *Durga*; we, kids included, gorged ourselves on all sorts of Indian snacks and treats and meals.

In that regard, Lily and Kate are (surprisingly) working on the south Asian single-seating record for tandoori chicken and buttered naan as well as consuming a meaningful quantity of butter chicken on the side, and I discovered a heavenly west Bengali chicken dish that rivals just about anything I've eaten so far... *in my life*.

And all of this happened relatively easily, in a city that we thought would be tremendously challenging. Christel even personally accompanied us to each site and helped us understand what we were seeing and experiencing. (She was married to a west Bengali and is really knowledgeable about Indian culture and food and language and religious persuasions, amongst other things.)

The truth is that our experience in Delhi was a bit sanitized, but in a good way. It is a monstrous city that is intimidating and crowded and dirty and foreign and congested and loud and beautiful and heartbreaking and exciting and happy and difficult. Moving around can sometimes be near impossible, even with a driver. Begging—sometimes aggressive and belligerent (desperate?) begging—is everywhere. And the girls are constantly, *constantly*, stopped for photographs and general petting and pinching. (It turns out that these Indians are just as interested in our simple clothes and blond hair as we are in their bright *sarees* and golden piercings and other markings.)

Delhi can be a frustrating place, even with the driver and guide and apartment with which we were provided. The bottom line is that we had a (very) good time and saw more than we ever would have without them.

(Oh, I have a great story about searching high and low for a bottle of wine and a couple beers one night alone on the backstreets and alleys of Delhi. When I finally found the hooch, I, a very interesting outsider, was pushed to the front of a long line, whisked behind a dirty counter and offered premium booze that appeared, well, let's just say that I don't think an official distributor had sold it to the fine establishment I stumbled upon. Then I was raucously cheered by around thirty drunkards for choosing large beers over small ones. At one point, I thought I was going to be mugged by the unruly crowd. It was a great experience: I was like a rock-star or national hero, all for doing something I've done far too often in my life. Picking the big beer. Fantastic.)

We are loving (and cursing) India so far. It is an inspiring place, and we can't wait to see what's next as we head off for points south: First Agra and the *Taj Mahal*, then Jaipur, the *Pink City* in the Land of Kings, then the beaches of Goa and eventually the backwaters of Kerala and Kochi (we think).

Very cool.

———•—

Nevertheless, like I said at the outset, it was bound to happen eventually. We genuinely miss home. It would be dishonest to suggest otherwise. But at the same time, we continue to have a wonderful time together, exploring new and different parts of the world.

Quite the conflict is brewing.

So as our nightly conversations drift from coffee machines to friends to western toilets and showers to everything else that makes California our home, we also excitedly discuss all we've done and seen in the past months and each new day's experiences and hardships and surprises. And in the course of those conversations, Wendi and I have figured something important out for ourselves, I think, something that makes what we are doing all the more fun and meaningful.

It turns out that there is an unanticipated, serendipitous side benefit to all this traveling business.

We suddenly find ourselves just as enamored with the idea of coming home—and doing all the things we once saw as the (increasingly mundane) day-to-day routine—as we are with traveling the world with our kids. We now see that the trip won't end the day we fly home, but rather will be sort of half-over. We're excited to get settled back in and find a job or open a business and take the girls to school and walk the dog and take out the trash and meet friends for drinks and generally live our life again. And we are anxiously awaiting the time we'll spend reconnecting with friends and family and doing all the things we love so much. We can only hope that it will be as fun for all of them as it will undoubtedly be for us.

Namaste, friends. We have more to see and to do.

But we'll see you soon.

CHAPTER 27
MOTHER INDIA

Agonda Beach, India
November 2011

---

*India was the motherland of our race, and Sanskrit the
mother of Europe's languages; she was the mother of our
philosophy; mother, through the Arabs, of much of our math-
ematics; mother, through the Buddha, of the ideals embodied
in Christianity; mother, through the village community, of
self-government and democracy. Mother India is in many
ways the mother of us all.*
—William J. Durant,
American historian and philosopher

---

*W*HAT THE...?!
      I had just started to fall asleep in the front seat of the
Tata Indica eV2 we were taking from Delhi to Agra (what,
you've never heard of the *Indica eV2?*) and was lost somewhere
between the realms of the restful and the restless when I was
abruptly brought back to the real world as we swerved hard
left and then back to the right, causing my head to slam against
the window beside me.

My eyes parted and I saw a seemingly impossible scene
unfolding through the soft light and smog and mist of the
early morning.

There was an overturned grain cart in the middle of the road with a few bulls wandering aimlessly around it and groups of people squatting everywhere, sweeping up the spilt load with homemade broom-thingys. There was a large truck flashing its brights and coming straight at us on the wrong side of the road and moving fast. As we bobbed and weaved through all that, we nearly hit a camel that was pulling a cart with a man in a turban sleeping on it.

There were scooters and rickshaws and cars everywhere, in no apparent order. People spilled out into the lanes—not a freeway as you and I know one, but more of an early version of a potholed country road in serious disrepair—from a roadside market that sold everything from fruits and vegetables to cell phones to livestock and hair products.

A serious accident was imminent.

Our driver was inexplicably *accelerating*, explaining nonchalantly that people often travel long distances on camels and sleep as they go since the camel "knows its way," while he deftly maneuvered the *Indica eV2* through the whole mess on the dirt and sand far off the shoulder. My knuckles were white from the death-grip I had on the door handle. I saw Wendi's eyes go from large to huge to moon-like in the rearview mirror. None of us were even wearing seatbelts.

The kids slept soundly through the whole thing.

Welcome to India.

We'd seen it in Delhi, of course, but like I said in *Thoughts of Home*, our experience there felt a bit sanitized. It turned out to be a warm-up for things to come. After our driver safely navigated the aforementioned apocalyptic scene straight out of *Road Warrior*, I stayed awake and watched the sun rise. And as it did, Mother India yawned lazily, opened her eyes and stretched out before us. She revealed herself to us unapologetically, unabashedly ... and relentlessly.

"Behold," she said. "I am India. I will overwhelm all of your senses and confuse you and inspire you and frustrate you and I will love you and your kids. I will comfort you. I will cause you discomfort, too, but I will not harm you. I am beautiful and sensuous but I can be ugly and unforgiving as well. And you will love me for it."

She was right.

India is lots of things, none of which I claim to understand in any meaningful way. My gut is that it would take most westerners—myself included—a lifetime to accumulate real insight into Indian culture and thought and religion and society and economics and business and philosophy and everything else happening on the subcontinent. There is much going on here, shaped by centuries of tradition and ritual and foreign invasion and conquest and myriad other influential forces.

And so, rather than try to reason my way through it all, I thought I would just put together a few illustrative *vignettes* in an effort to convey what's going down here, at least as we've seen it. I hope you'll enjoy them and, perhaps, get a feel for our collective experience.

It's the best I can do.

Oh, and since *vignette* is technically defined by *Merriam-Webster* as "a short descriptive literary sketch," I am going to limit myself to just 250 words per description. Given my propensity to ramble on and on without end (trust me, what you read here is typically a heavily redacted version of what I start with), this should be, well, *challenging*. In fact, I may better find myself able to satisfy the less restrictive standard set forth in *The Free Dictionary*'s definition of *vignette*: "A short, *usually* descriptive literary sketch [emphasis added]."

Anywho, here goes.

India the Beautiful

My (brilliant) aunt called it a "mirage." That may very well be the best one-word description I can think of and I'd love to steal it, but I won't. Instead, I'll go with a love story forged of marble set on the serene *Yamuna River* on the outskirts of the otherwise chaotic ancient city of Agra. (I can already tell that I will never make 250 words. I really need to dump some of those adjectives and ... *ands*.)

Either way, the *Taj Mahal* is a remarkable structure. It is immediately and universally familiar, yet nevertheless evokes a unique, visceral reaction from the time you see it far off in the distance to the time you cross the vast south garden, climb the stairs, float across an expanse of soft white marble and enter the simple yet elegant tomb of *Shah Jahan* and his wife, *Mumtaz Mahal*.

The whole scene is surreal yet powerfully emotional, and as you run your fingers over the ornate inscriptions and patterns made of precious stones and circle the intricately carved and pierced marble screen (or *jali*), which encompasses the burial places of the Emperor and Empress, you can actually feel *Jahan's* torment and mourning that served as the foundation for the design and construction of the mausoleum after his beloved *Mahal* tragically died.

The *Taj Mahal* took more than 22 years and 20,000 workers, including literally thousands of women hauling earth in trays on their heads in alternating shifts, day and night, for years, to complete. Ancient India's finest craftsmen were summoned from the far corners of the empire and came together to create what is perhaps the most visually stunning monument we have seen to date. In fact, seeing it from across the *Yamuna* at sunset—with colorful locals on the river banks, their candles and fires burning brightly—is a moving experience that is worth seeking out. In a word, the *Taj Mahal* is amazing.

India the beautiful.

(*Damnit man!* 302 words, excluding the narrative parenthetical at the end of the first paragraph, and I didn't even get the chance to explain that there are at least some (pessimistic) people out there who say that the *Taj Mahal* is not quite the love story I think it is. Those (negative, terrible) people would say that *Jahan*, an egomaniac, built it for himself.

But that's no fun and I refuse to believe it.

I also didn't get to say that there is a legend that the whole structure takes its shape from the contours of a woman and that the domes are designed from the shape of a woman's breast. If I had said all that, I'd have been up to around 400 words, a full sixty percent over the target. Pathetic effort.)

India the Frustrating (or India the Sleeping Giant)

In our months of travel, we have learned that driving through countries or cities can be a wonderful way to get a feel for them and really see what is happening from a bigger picture perspective. (Nothing beats simply wandering the streets on foot and mingling with the locals, of course, but seeing vast areas from the car provides a different view that is meaningful too.) India has been perhaps the best example of this.

The road from Delhi to Agra really revealed, to me, anyway, India's challenges and its potential. We repeatedly witnessed what is a stunning mass migration, one that happens every single day. There is an endless biomass of people and animals and crops and foodstuffs moving along the highway, and its volume is truly shocking. And it all moves together in every conceivable mode of transportation, in a largely disorganized and frankly inefficient manner. This leads to monster traffic jams with cars and motorcycles and people and bicycles and scooters and rickshaws and auto-rickshaws and oxen and horse-drawn carts and bulls roaming around all on bad or terrible roads without meaningful traffic signals or laws. (There's all those darn *ands* again.)

In other words, the whole scene resembles total chaos that might stretch for miles and miles under a very hot Indian sun.

The pollution levels are staggering, and you can see the ubiquitous heavy smog in many of the pictures we took. The whole thing is sometimes frustrating, sometimes funny, and always amazing to watch. Even when you're stuck in it.

This was the same scene we saw unfold on the road from Agra to Jaipur and on the streets of each and every city we've visited in India. Delhi's roads could be completely shut down by these migrations; Agra was almost completely impassable when we arrived; the streets of Jaipur's *Pink City* were clogged and polluted too.

India the frustrating.

India the Sleeping Giant, though, too.

(*Damnit again!* That's already over 300 words—again excluding the narrative parenthetical in the middle of the second paragraph—and I'm not even close to done yet. This is embarrassing.)

The country is enormously populated, with more than 1.2 billion people in an area that is approximately one-third the size of the continental United States. When the riddle that is India is finally solved—and it will be, eventually—and people move more freely, more efficiently, and are even better educated (they already are a fairly learned bunch), they will comprise a powerful labor force that will demand to be recognized.

In other words, if you think "offshoring" is bad now, just wait. I'm no doomsday apocalyptic type but my gut is that there won't be many jobs left for our highly paid and increasingly less educated workers when developing nations like India successfully mobilize their vast human resources and unlock their full potential.

The next fifty years will be interesting, trust me.

Oh, I can't help myself. Here's a funny yet sad anecdote. I was sitting in the office of a very senior lawyer many years ago in San Francisco and we were talking through some of the problems that faced a very large Detroit car manufacturer my firm represented. At the end of the conversation, the lawyer, a friend, said something like, "The only chance for your children, Matt, and my grandchildren, will be to export the American legal system to all of these developing nations and peoples. That will drive up labor costs, as it has done here and elsewhere already, and give our kids a chance to compete."

The funny thing is that it was two American lawyers sitting around talking about it. The sad thing is that old Sam Miller may have been right.

(Even excluding my frustrated parenthetical and ill-advised anecdote, that's nearly 430 words, not even close. I'll do my best to make up for it in the next couple, I swear.)

India the Amazing

There are few places we've been that offer such a wide array of experiences as those which exist here in India. There are many examples of this diversity but perhaps the best one came just a few days ago in a twelve-hour stretch in Jaipur.

We started the day with a simple plan to see the *Amber Fort*, one of a number of hilltop fortresses that dot the mountains around north India. (To us, the best one was just up the *Yamuna* from the *Taj Mahal* in Agra, but I digress.) When we got to the parking area at the bottom of the hill, we saw that you could rent an elephant with a colorful wooden couch strapped to its back to walk you to the top.

Clearly something we couldn't pass up.

We took a picture I like to look at that shows all of us just before hopping on. There's a gleeful, carefree look in my wife and children's eyes that I simply love.

But that disappeared very quickly, yielding to wide-eyed grimaces of sheer terror once we got going.

We got THAT ELEPHANT. You know, the old one that doesn't really want to be carting tourists around all day. He's thinking about playing golf and drinking *piña coladas* through his nose in the desert somewhere, retired, living the good life. He's just not into the whole "I'm a happy worker" employment thing anymore.

And so he started slowly, lumbering up the hill. We were immediately and frequently passed by other cheerful people riding other cheerful elephants with smiling drivers simply sitting, peacefully, just behind their respective elephant's heads and doing little else. Compare that, if you will, to our comparably aging driver, who soon lost his patience with the gigantic (and clearly disagreeable) beast underneath us and began screaming and beating our ride mercilessly.

Pleasant experience, especially for the kids' first time.

(Note that I saved only fun photographs of this traumatic time in an effort to dull the nightmarish stress and anxiety that will inevitably come when my wife and daughters and I feel safe enough to read this and relive our fifteen minutes of hell on the back of an elephant. I digress.)

At one point, our driver was literally standing on the elephant's head and smashing his knee or foot into the back of the giant cranium. The elephant, not surprisingly, did not like this behavior, and began trying to turn around in the narrow but excruciatingly long stone road on which he labored. There was a five foot wall protecting us from a large and very steep cliff on the downhill side, and the fifteen foot animal would get close and turn toward it, as if contemplating his own mortality and worth in an unjust world. Then he would stop, consider sitting, endure some beating and screaming, and set forth again, reluctantly.

They seem ridiculous now, but these are the types of things that ran through my mind as I alternatively tried to comfort the girls—Lily was truly terrified, almost to the point of tears—and begged my wife to calm herself in front of the children:

C'mon Matt, think! How many cases of elephant suicide have you read about? Will this thing actually go berserk and scale the wall and just jump with all of us on its back? I remember reading that elephants are smart and empathetic… won't he think of us before acting so recklessly? What about the circus "accidents" you see in the news from time to time?

Dear god you moron, stop berating the damn thing, it might actually understand you! And enough with the savage beating of the powerful, massive beast that could crush us all should he choose! We are not in control, man, the elephant can do whatever he wants! Assuage him, fool! Placate him!

You know, things like that.

We did eventually make it to the top and dismount, saving our lives and, perhaps, our marriage. I accidently laughed right in the driver's face when he asked for a tip.

He was not amused.

(Forget it. *Vignettes* just aren't my thing. But I will do my best to be brief from here on out.)

We explored the fort and had a quick drink in the restaurant at the top that has been designed like an ancient palace (really cool, not too "touristy"). Then we walked down—no, we didn't try another elephant—and came across a snake charmer.

Terrific.

I'm pretty much what you'd think of as a snake-hater, but my wonderful wife coerced me into sitting next to the guy for a little show (hmmm... payback for the elephant experience?). Let's just say that I was *uncomfortable*, and eventually as terrified as Lily was up on the elephant. Frankly, it was not a particularly fun or pleasant experience.

The truth is that I hate all snakes and the men who claim to charm them. I recognize full-well that this is an indefensible generalization against a minority population that bears the hallmarks of bigotry. But I stand by it. Proudly.

After that, we had to rush across town to pick up a new friend, Robert, the lawyer-turned-clothes-designer we'd met at the hotel the day before. He had invited us a *puja* at his Indian manufacturer's house and we eagerly accepted. We made it just in time and walked into a full blown Hindu religious festival meant to clean the house and those in it of any bad stuff (my understanding).

There were Hindu idols beautifully decorated with marigolds and other flowers positioned carefully, there were hours of chanting and singing holy texts, there was a guru—a real guru!—blessing people, there was incense and dancing and flower petals thrown everywhere and tons of other cool stuff. (There were no snakes. Thank you *Shiva*.)

The guru not only blessed my forehead but also offered me a perfumed bit of cotton to tuck into my ear and blessed a few bananas since the focus of the *puja* was the Monkey God who helped *Rama* rescue his perfect wife *Sita* from an evil Sri Lankan kidnapper by building a bridge made of all the monkeys in south India to Sri Lanka.

Long story, trust me, and I was made to understand that it is the genesis of tension between India and, you guessed it, Sri Lanka (again, my understanding).

Tons of delicious food were prepared for the 400-person party that followed and everybody was happy and smiling; it was a real celebration of life that featured very accessible gods and smiling prominent religious figures who were happy to talk. (Compare that to the strict western church many of us know; worlds apart, really.) Very cool experience, even if we didn't understand much of what was happening. Lily and Kate really loved the whole thing and danced and sang and threw marigolds and rose petals all afternoon. What a day.

India the Amazing.

India the Paradise

We now find ourselves taking a break on *Agonda Beach* in Goa. We are living in a simple hut on the sand. The Arabian Sea is fifty feet away. The air is humid, around ninety degrees. The water is warm and saline, around eighty degrees. There are few people and not many things to do beyond read, walk the beach, lie in the sand or spend hours playing in the water. The locals are curious and friendly.

We are quite a distance off the beaten path here, in a place where the jungle meets the sand and the sea and few roads can carry you in or out.

A walk down the beach might reveal a few bulls, women in *sarees* standing in the water, dunking their children (religious? simple bathing?), a few people meditating or doing yoga or just spending the afternoon sleeping in the powdery sand near the water's edge, others building more huts for the high season that has technically already started (but you wouldn't know that from the looks of things). After the walk, you might order a freshly squeezed and blended orange or pineapple or mango or one of other mouthwatering juices they twist up at the restaurant in front of our hut. Fresh fish and fantastic Indian dishes for which you'd pay dozens of dollars (or more) per plate in the States cost around three dollars.

This is a special place. And I doubt that there are many like it in the world.

India the Paradise.

Mother India.

(*Success!* 250 words on the dot. I'd guess better quit while I'm ahead. And besides, the sea is calling.)

CHAPTER 28
SCHIZTOPHRENIA
(OR LET'S GET PHYSICAL)

Agonda Beach, India
November 2011

Who are you?
—The Who

I HAVE A CONFESSION to make.

It's not a big deal, you know, nothing I can't handle. But it's starting to take up an abnormally large percentage of my time and I can't seem to stop *doing it*. Or maybe it's that I don't *want* to stop doing it.

It just feels so good.

It's yoga, man, and I'm pretty into it. Like, um, I like it.

A lot.

Before I go any further, I suppose I should make a very large, very broad disclaimer in an effort to protect against any potential harm to my personal and/or professional reputation. I made my living, after all, as a business litigator and advisor for nearly eight full years before I took off with my family for some well-deserved quality time. I was a reasonable lawyer, not a bare-knuckle brawler but one who prided himself on really seeing the big picture and making recommendations that not only forwarded his clients' litigation interests but their business ones as well. I was able to be at least somewhat successful in that role because, ultimately, when the going got tough (as it inevitably would), I stood firm for my clients. I fought for them when there was something to fight for, and that alone—the willingness and ability to take it to the proverbial mat if need be—helped stave off much of the bull-poop that comes as part and parcel of having a successful business in the United States.

There's the tension.

I mean, come on, how would my clients' adversaries react if they knew that I was filling my time on some beach in India giggling at jokes from dreadlocked yoga instructors like "this is flower yoga, not power yoga" or doing my best to "surrender to" rather than "fight against" various poses that have me looking more like a ballet-dancer than a battle-hardened litigator? They'd start thinking they could push me around, beat me up, maybe even call me names, and that—for better or worse—would be the beginning of the end of my litigation career.

And so, in an effort to protect my livelihood and help ensure that I can continue to support my wife and daughters when the time comes, I hereby affirmatively declare, with full confidence and conviction, that I am still the same lawyer I was when I left Santa Barbara more than five months ago. Please don't misunderstand or misinterpret any of that which follows to signify any fundamental change in my thinking or my ability. I can still get it done when it needs to get done.

Don't worry.

It's just that I've been living in this hut on *Agonda Beach* for many, many days now. You'd think I'd be going nuts sharing a one room shack with three (admittedly beautiful) women but I'm not. I'm actually enjoying it. We wake to the sound of waves crashing on the beach, leisurely rise and dress in bathing suits and shuffle to breakfast at a small place on the sand or maybe the little bakery up the single lane road that runs parallel to the water. No shirt, no shoes (and perhaps no pants, but we haven't tested that) required. We stroll back along the water, dipping our toes and making patterns in the sand.

Then I typically take the girls swimming, which provides hours of entertainment. To be honest, I didn't know how the kids would react to the whole third-world tropical scene—there is basically nothing to do here—but I shouldn't have been worried. Warm water and warm air and big empty beaches are enough fun to last quite awhile. We've made up games like "*Water Moose*" (this is the one where I get down on all fours and Lily and Kate climb onto my back on the sand and I lumber out into the waves, mooing and groaning loudly, until they are knocked off into the shore pound), "*Super Missile*" (I'm a human dart in this one, and I have to target the girls and then bodysurf into them, ramming them down into the whitewash) and "*Let's Go Fly a Kite*" (I'm like a beached whale here, rolling around in the impact zone and whitewash, while we basically scream *Let's Go Fly a Kite* from *Mary Poppins* repeatedly and without stopping for any reason as they try to climb on top of me and hold on while waves knock us all over the place. That's probably their favorite lately).

The fun is only amplified when my wife saunters down and plays along. (She's my favorite target in *Super Missile*.) The good news is that I've swallowed enough salt water to ensure a healthy intestinal and colon cleansing, which is a real side benefit to all the horsing around.

At some point, one of us suggests some down time, so we drag ourselves up the beach and over the hot sand to the lounge chairs in front of our hut and order a round of fresh pineapple or watermelon juices (or the occasional pre-noon *Kingfisher*, a delightful Indian beer). Wendi and I generally read while the kids play around us in the sand. Sometimes we really marshal our collective strength and build a sandcastle modeled after the *Taj Mahal* or one of the forts we've seen in India. You get the idea.

Then it's lunchtime—say, a prawn curry or chicken vindaloo or maybe even a baked whole fish to share, done tandoori-style—then a nap back in the hut. We wake whenever, usually due to palm fronds rustling in the afternoon breeze. More swimming, maybe *"Under Over Class"* (a pretend school in the water, where the kids decide whether to go over or under each wave and we talk about whether they got it right or not).

Sunset comes pretty quickly from there, and we take a walk or sit around and watch the whole thing go down. The sunsets have been invariably gorgeous, and we tend not to talk too much as we watch the sky turn the colors of a bonfire while the bright fiery orange ball sinks lower and lower into the Arabian Sea.

There's a pick-up cricket game right in front of our hut each evening, and I've taken to playing every now and then. The local guys get a kick out of my American baseball style, and I tease them about not being able to throw right or "hit the long ball." They offer me *paan* to chew on—a mild (but effective!) stimulant consisting of areca nut and some sort of lime paste and some spices, I think, wrapped in a betel leaf (think of baseball players and chewing tobacco, I suppose, except with a bright red spit byproduct instead of a gritty brown one)—while we play and laugh and joke around like guys playing hardball back home might.

It's soon time for dinner so we rinse in our outdoor shower and wander around, looking for a new best place or going back to an old favorite. (By the way, our experience has been that Indian food is terrific and generally safe, loved even by the kiddies.) We put the girls to bed and Wendi and

I stay up talking or reading or playing cards on our porch. Sometimes we just go to bed with the girls and giggle for awhile before we all fall asleep. Deep sleep comes easy here (we splurged and have an air-conditioner and a fan in our hut ... otherwise, things might be different). Morning seems to come quickly.

And then we do it all again.

That's it.

Except, of course, for the yoga. There are these wonderful yoga classes each and every morning, and Wendi and I have been trading off. One is right down the beach, just off the sand, under a canopy of coconut palms backed by bright blue skies. A British ex-pat (the aforementioned dreadlocked instructor) teaches a 90-minute class that takes you everywhere from downward facing dog—oh, I mean *Adho Mukha Svanasana*—to full headstands and other contortions that may only be possible for us mere mortals because our bodies are warm from the gentle tropical heat.

There's another class just across the road from us that goes down amongst the palms on the top of a three story yoga school. It's pretty advanced and really flows in and out of every imaginable pose—it is actually used to teach neophyte yoga instructors lots of techniques—for a couple hours. It's a strenuous endeavor, to say the least, and it is absolutely amazing to see real yogic gurus at work in their craft. The power and grace and focus is truly unbelievable.

And there I am, right in the middle of it, board shorts and topless, huffing and puffing and sweating (profusely) and struggling to even attempt half of what others seem to do so effortlessly. And I love it.

I love the whole damn thing.

I love the breathing and the chilling and the meditation. I love the time for personal reflection and release. I love seeing new parts of my body, ones I've never even seen before, as I reach and bend and twist (as much as possible, anyway, for a "tight white guy," as I've become known around here). I love seeing the world from all sorts of different perspectives. *(Is that an upside-down palm tree I see under my right thigh? Wait. Is that even my right thigh? What part of my body is that?)* I love the singular focus and the shutting out, for a little while, of everything else. I love the ubiquitous heavy breathing meditation—oh, excuse me, I mean *prananyama*—that finds its way into each class. I love the rested and peaceful feeling that permeates *my soul* (yeah, my soul) when the whole thing is said and done.

I don't mean to go on forever here, but you know what I love most? Two things. First, the beginning sort of "getting in touch with your body, taking a mental inventory of stress or soreness or injury" part of the class. Second, the ending sort of "lie there like a corpse and strive for total relaxation," maybe do some visualization, maybe send some "healing vibes" to a sore knee or elbow.

I'm still right there, man, like...I don't know, watching myself with my third eye, flying over magical lands or wandering in a vast desert or hanging in an ice fortress far away from everything. Feeling the difference in temperature between the pinky toe on my right foot and the big toe on my left. Feeling my body fully relax and sink into a very supportive Mother Earth. Whatever. Stuff like that. Love it.

Laugh if you want. It's not about vanity or competition so I don't care. I'm into it. Period.

I walk back to the hut from the class feeling fantastic. I'm smiling, I'm relaxed, I'm peaceful. My mind feels super clear and focused and I'm ready to tackle the day that lies ahead. And I actually, consciously want to do it in a balanced and healthy way.

That's a long way, trust me, from the coffee-drenched maniac I was each morning a few months ago. That Matt—Old Matt, for convenience—would hammer an *Eggs Benedict* (extra bacon and fill up that bottomless coffee!) and then crank through each busy morning, adding chores to a massive to-do list as quickly as he checked them off. Old Matt might sometimes get out for a run along East Beach, but he would actually *take his phone with him and answer calls and emails as he went.* (I know, it's obscene.) Old Matt usually got home for dinner, but not always, and the phone never stopped vibrating loudly in the next room.

Old Matt might even put the kids to bed and then go back to the office to finish a few things up.

Old Matt seems like a pretty hard core dude, especially when viewed through the (admittedly foggy) lens of hindsight here in Goa.

New Matt, the one that lives and breathes today in India, glides through a yoga class in the morning and comes back to the hut for a *masala chai* and *muesli* (I didn't even know what that was a few months ago, seriously) with milk and honey. Then he writes a bit as the kids finish homeschool before a family game of *Water Moose* or *Super Missile*. New Matt goes for a barefooted beach run, passing oxen and hippies deep in meditation and yogis flowing through their *asana* as he goes, listening to the *Grateful Dead* without a smartphone within a thousand miles. (I'm really cranking through the miles to *Shakedown Street* and *China Cat Sunflower* and *Truckin*; never thought that possible but it's distinctly true.) New Matt sits and enjoys dinners and lunches without much or any distraction. New Matt exercises patience with his kids and is a bit gentler, a bit calmer.

New Matt is good. Yes. I like New Matt.

I don't know, maybe these wild hippies of *Agonda Beach*

are right. Maybe I should measure my day in smiles and rainbows and sunshine rather than cases won and clients satisfied and money earned. Maybe I should start focusing on my yoga "practice" and retain this sense of calm and peace that took me five months and thousands of miles and a few dozen *vinyasas* to achieve.

Maybe I should say goodbye to Old Matt.

Forever.

New Matt is good. Yes. New Matt is good.

Hey, that sounds like a mantra...

Wait a second, what am I saying? Get a hold of yourself, man! *Snap out of it for Christ's sake!*

Clients, *friends*, as I was saying, I stand before you with full confidence and conviction. I am the same lawyer I was five months ago. I will still meet and exceed the business and litigation goals we set and will still stand firm to protect your interests. Don't worry, nobody will push me around. Nobody will call me names.

Nobody.

Except maybe my guru.

New Matt is good. New Matt is good. New Matt is good...

CHAPTER 29
DR. FEELGOOD

Fort Kochi, India
December 2011

Moon River...
—Irwin M. Fletcher

M OST MEN WHO GREW UP in relatively rural areas of northern
California, like I did, talk a lot about country music
and hunting and fishing and high school sports (and often
truly disturbing under-age drinking). And while I have a
few great fishing stories and a classic hunting tale that
involves me and my brother-in-law and a couple turkeys
and a wild night up in Lake County, my youth in Santa Rosa
and Sonoma and Napa Counties taught me something else
too. Something a little more refined, perhaps, and a little
less, well, *macho*.

I love spa days. Always have.

From my first mud bath with my high school sweetheart
at *Dr. Wilkinson's* in Calistoga when I was fifteen to the last
time—not all that long ago, actually—my wife and I spent a
long weekend enjoying beautiful food and drink and massages
and steam baths. I can't help it, man, I'm a sucker for that kind

of thing. I mean, give me a glass of champagne and a long dry sauna before a couple hours of general pampering ending with a tight full-body wrap, mint-infused water, cucumber slices on my eyes and a long snooze in a quiet room with, say, the gentle sounds of nature playing softly, and I am pretty much the happiest straight guy around. Seriously.

And so, given my long (happy) spa history and general propensity to enjoy all related things, my experience a few days ago was truly troubling.

Truly troubling indeed.

I had booked what I thought was a fairly routine few hours of relaxation bliss. But as I stared down at the triangle of white cotton on the round wood table in front of me, I was puzzled, concerned even. I wasn't totally sure what I was looking at or what I had gotten myself into. It was like that self-conscious first massage, all those years ago.

Am I supposed to COMPLETELY undress? And then get UNDER the sheet on the table? Face up or face down? What exactly is going on here?

It was that damned cotton triangle that caused all the confusion. I'd never seen anything like it. Its apex had been stretched way out, causing it to look quite like a flat, one-dimensional dunce cap. There was a piece of string made of twisted coconut fibers protruding from each side of its small base that was long enough to be tied around my waist, like a waiter's apron.

What the hell was I supposed to do with it?

I had undressed, like one would for any massage, and stood alone in the small room, pondering how best to approach the riddle in front of me.

"This is a test," I thought. *"Or maybe there was a miscommunication. It looks more like a blind-fold than a loin cloth. Maybe..."*

I marshaled all of my spa experience and weighed my options, trying hard not to harsh my pre-massage mellow. Ultimately, I figured that there was more risk in tying the damned thing around my head and emerging buck-naked and totally blind than there was going in eyes wide-open with an elongated cotton triangle protecting my, ah, *situation*.

I like consistency. So I thought it best to pass the point of the triangle back through my legs and tie it up against my lower back with the coconut rope. Sort of like an emaciated sumo wrestler. Or, I suppose, like a very fashionable woman in the latest hip-style of south Asian G-string.

Take your pick.

Once I had completed the frankly challenging tying process, I was convinced that I had it right. (And I did; nobody was as surprised as I was, trust me.) Disaster avoided, I surveyed the dim room and saw all sorts of implements of relaxation. Oils warming on a small stove, colorful powders ground and mixed in stone mortars, flowers floating in golden bowls (similar to the one described back in *The Curse of the Tibetan Healing Bowl*), candles and incense set ablaze. There was music of an unknown origin playing softly from invisible speakers. I sat down in an ancient chair next to a beautiful wooden massage table.

A man walked through the door and bowed.

Let me say that again: *A man* walked through the doors and bowed.

Not the happiest straight guy around in that particular moment. In fact, it may be more accurate to say that I was the most *uncomfortable* or even *panicked* straight guy around at that moment. But I was quickly able to regain my composure, for I knew something.

Something important.

This man was no ordinary masseuse, he was a doctor.

And this was no ordinary massage, it was a uniquely Indian form of medicine that has been around for over 5000 years.

My new physician approached confidently, with a tool that resembled both a paintbrush and an ancient Asian weapon. I closed my eyes. I breathed deep.

And, much as I had back in that *hamam* in Istanbul, I awaited my fate.

—•—

It wasn't like I needed an extensive Ayurvedic treatment. After all, we'd spent the past week relaxing and generally enjoying life in and around Fort Kochi in the southwestern Indian state of Kerala. But in my quest to reach a resting heart rate of three beats per minute, I thought I'd give it a try.

We left *Agonda Beach* on an overnight train bound for Fort Kochi on Thanksgiving. We spent our holiday relaxed, at a mind-blowing vegetarian restaurant in the Goan jungle and then gobbling Tandoori Chicken and potatoes—not mashed but French fried (it was the best we could do)—on the sand, giving thanks for Indian beaches and hospitality and for friends and family thousands of miles away. I'd become pretty cozy with the pick-up beach cricket gang over our couple weeks at *Agonda*, and they surprised me after dinner with a thoughtful gesture.

They secretly pooled their rupees and bought a soccer ball—knowing that I preferred *futbol* to cricket—and we knocked it around in a spirited game on the hard-packed sand at low tide on the Arabian Sea until the moment we left in a cab bound for a small Indian train station, when the sun sank slowly into the water.

It was hard to walk away from the hut and the yoga and the sunsets and the new friends and the simple existence there in Goa. Very hard.

In another life, I may have missed that train and stayed right there, right then, forever.

But southern India beckoned. Our cab ride took us over nearly impassable narrow dirt roads, away from the beach and deep into a "spooky forest"—Lily's description and perfectly accurate—with deformed old-growth trees covered in moss and ferns and vines and eerie and unfamiliar animal calls and a full moon and witches on broomsticks and black cats and graveyards (maybe). It was the kind of night drive that sets a kid's imagination on fire and it was fun for all of us to look out the windows and see what we could see.

When we reached the station, we learned that our train was behind schedule. *Four hours* behind schedule. And so we spent the last hours of our holiday on a hard and not particularly clean stone bench, covered with bags and my guitar, still sandy from *Agonda*, stuck in some train depot somewhere in south Goa.

Happy Thanksgiving.

With that said, the experience of hanging around a remote Indian train station late at night was actually pretty cool. And let me tell you, the experience of traveling on an overnight train in India is nothing at all like traveling on an overnight train from, say, Madrid to Lisbon. Quite different, in fact.

But we were lucky and had some (very limited) space and a few benches—er, ah, beds—in an area with a group of progressive Indian students who were quick to smile and generally accommodate us. The ride was rough, super loud, with the train windows open the whole way and fans on high blowing air in every direction and people stacked on top of people with more people beside them and below them and babies crying and men smoking between cars all night.

I didn't get much sleep but the kids did, and, from over my novel, I could see that Wendi got a few hours of shut eye too. It was romantic in a funny kind of way, one of those experiences you never forget. I loved it.

We reached Fort Kochi in the late-morning and immediately liked it. Many people say it, and we found it to be true: South India is a far different place than north India. It almost feels like an entirely different country. Slower, more relaxed, perhaps more hospitable, softer. It felt great, even despite the fact that we truly enjoyed our time in Delhi and environs. We were glad to be there, right away, and we weren't forced to speed up too quickly after maybe the mellowest two + weeks of my life at *Agonda Beach*. Perfect.

Fort Kochi has, at various times in its history, been controlled by the Dutch or the Portuguese (or the British) as a strategically important location for the lucrative spice trade, so it is a cool old colonial-type place. It's also very tropical, with heavy air and lots of the same types of old-growth trees that we saw in the "spooky forest" mentioned above.

It's a bit mysterious too, if you look carefully, away from relatively touristy Princess Street. It's the kind of place where people believe in and occasionally see ghosts, where candles on concrete ledges are still surreptitiously lit each night and offered with flowers (and sometimes liquor) to spirits of African slaves who were brutally killed in the mid-1600's after their (conquered) Portuguese "owners" left them behind to fend for themselves against the (conquering) Dutch.

You know, stuff like that.

It's funny, but when you're in a place like this and see that the local folks are gravely serious, you become serious too. No need to tempt fate and risk bumping into *Kappiri Muthappan* or one of the other slaves in some dark Indian alley late at night. No way, no sir. I'd rather leave a shot of whiskey and some flowers and show some respect and gratitude. Straight up.

There is a lot to do around Fort Kochi and Kerala, generally, and we made time to do at least some of it at a very casual pace. The town itself is an attraction, and we spent days just wandering it and eating great meals and meeting people, *et cetera*. We spent an hour or two watching fishermen lower and raise and lower and raise the giant ancient *Chinese Fishing Nets* that dot the beaches; pretty cool, actually, and the related fish market is a fun place to hang out and watch the crowds argue fervently over price or quantity or whatever.

We bought our way into a fancy hotel's pool one day and hung out and swam. Wendi got a massage. Time passed.

I took a *hatha* yoga class one morning and spent a full hour deep in meditation while listening to a live sitar and Indian drum act perform an ancient *raga*—some say that these *ragas*, performed and heard properly, can heal and perform other miracles—with a very international group of (wildly) eccentric hippies and others, some of whom were clearly searching for an alternative cure, perhaps for something deemed incurable in the western world.

It was heart-breaking and uplifting and real. It was the kind of thing that helps a thirty-six-year-old put into crystal-clear focus the things in life that are meaningful and the things in life that are not. I spent my hour thinking about those kinds of things and listening to the music, and then I walked back to our room and spent the day playing with my wife and kids.

We caught a *Kathakali* production one night in a classic old theater, and enjoyed watching the players—all men—go through a painstakingly long and intricate pre-stage make-up and costuming process. The show was the story of the death of *Kichaka Katti*, a royal who had unknowingly but quite aggressively and violently (bordering on totally inappropriate for the children) pursued the wife of an exiled prince. There were no words spoken by the actors; the story was told by a singer and a group of musicians and the players' complex hand movements and precise facial expressions. It was a form of theater none of us had ever seen and we had a blast.

The kids especially loved the end, and giggled uncontrollably when *Kichaka Katti* was finally caught and stabbed (again, bordering on completely inappropriate, we know) and died slowly and loudly on the stage. Their unabashed pleasure at the sight of violent death concerned Wendi and me quite a bit and we were seriously questioning our parental judgment; at least until it became clear at a debriefing over dinner after the show that neither Lily nor Kate understood what exactly was going on.

Phew.

The next day, we woke early to take a tour of the beautiful Kerala backwaters, which twist and turn their way through uninhabited islands and remote villages and gorgeous scenery. We boarded a barge that had been used to transport rice throughout the region years ago and cruised up and down waterways for a couple hours before stopping at a small village where things haven't changed much in the past hundred years. We learned lots of interesting stuff about native plants and medicines and beliefs, but perhaps the most telling was that this group has been making "toddy"—a slightly to very potent alcoholic beverage that tastes not great and smells absolutely horrible—from sap taken from the flower of the coconut palm for centuries.

It soon dawned on me that these guys have been out here in the middle of nowhere making booze since the beginning of time. You just have to wonder about the first guy who figured all this out; was he called insane and persecuted for tipping back one too many magical potions? I bet he was, but only until the rest of the village caught on.

The bottom line is that man's drive and ingenuity, especially for making and ingesting a wide variety of intoxicants, is pretty incredible.

Sorry, distracting topic. Where was I?

Oh yes, the backwaters of Kerala.

We finished the day in an ancient Indian canoe with an ancient Indian gondolier, for lack of a better word (indeed, some call the backwaters of Kerala the "Venice of the East"), navigating ancient narrow canals surrounded by thick jungle and all that you'd expect to see out there. Snakes swimming alongside the canoe, small huts and villages from another time (we stopped for tea in one such village, although unlike the first place we visited, my gut is that this one had been recreated for us tourists), animals and insects of unknown providence chirping and buzzing and cawing from somewhere nearby under a hot sun in very humid conditions. We all really enjoyed it.

Kerala was great. It was a fantastic way to end our time in India. In many ways, it was a microcosm of our time in south Asia. A huge variety of experience, generally warm, friendly and hospitable people, beauty and struggle everywhere, happiness and sadness, ease and difficulty, wealth and poverty, all standing right beside one another.

We truly enjoyed the past month and a half, even if it wasn't always the easiest traveling.

We will return one day to experience more of it.

—•—

The good doctor painted some warm oil across my chest and upper back with his paintbrush, gently descending down my sternum and spine, respectively. Then he massaged my scalp and head, paying special attention to pressure points behind my ears and at the base of my skull. It was wonderful.

So wonderful, in fact, that I soon fell asleep.

I don't know much, but I do know that he spent a fair

amount of time on the palms of my hands and in between my fingers as well as on the bottoms of my feet and my toes. And my whole body—save those parts covered by the protective cotton dunce-cap—was slick with oil and felt great, healthy, clean and rejuvenated, when I came out of my coma.

I drifted through the rest of the day easily.

I'd like to tell you that I measured my resting heart rate and met my goal of three beats per minute, but I was too relaxed to do any such thing. And when my wife asked me what I thought of the Ayurvedic experience and whether I'd do it again, my affirmative answer came quickly.

Spa days may not be the most masculine thing on the planet, but what can I say?

I guess you can take the boy out of northern California.

But you can't take the northern California out of the boy.

CHAPTER 30
WORSHIPPING ELEPHANTS

Somewhere Outside of Fort Kochi, India
December 2011

Emancipate yourself from mental slavery,
None but ourselves can free our minds.
—Bob Marley

I KNOW I JUST WROTE about the end of our time in south Asia but we had a great experience on our very last night in Kerala that I really wanted to get down. We are presently at-large, somewhere between Fort Kochi and Chiang Mai, running like crazy to catch a variety of planes, trains and automobiles, so here's a quick one, written fast on airport benches, often with sleeping children draped over my lap.

There are certain experiences, certain moments, in each of our lives that simply cannot be forgotten or duplicated. These wrinkles in time can be had anywhere, anytime, of course, but the fact is that our little excursion has produced a steady stream of them that I—all of us, hopefully—will remember forever.

Some of those moments are memorable because they are shockingly horrifying, like the time when Kate, then three years old and genuinely astonished by the wonder that is a fine Italian gelato (her first), shouted *Nazi!* through a sugar-crazed grin at the woman behind the counter in a quiet but crowded parkside *gelateria*, rather than *Gratzie!*, as we had practiced so hard for weeks. (We've since cleared that up.)

Others are memorable for their purity and innocence, like when Lily whispered in my ear *"I can see the whole world from here, Daddy,"* as I held her close and we looked over Manhattan at sunset from the *Empire State Building* before we boarded our flight for Dublin all those months ago. Still others are unforgettable for their beauty, like my wife smiling on the *Rialto Bridge* in Venice in a waning light or relaxing, not knowing I could see her from afar, on a park bench in Paris watching the world pass by.

The list goes on and on.

For me, though, few places have produced so many indelible images as India, from the breathtaking view of the *Taj Mahal* from across the *Yamuna River* at sunset to the street scenes in Delhi and from the beaches of Goa to the backwaters of Kerala. It seems that all of our chins are badly bruised from the near-constant parade of jaw-dropping sights and smells and tastes set to the wild cacophony that seems to permeate every hour of every day here.

In a fitting end to our time in India, we spent our last night at *Sree Poornathrayeesa*, an ancient Hindu Temple outside of Fort Kochi, witnessing a mind-boggling festival focused on worshipping elephants with jewels and prayer and fire and music and food (according to me, anyway). Few tourists were present—we spotted only a couple in a crowd of thousands—and the whole scene was so fascinating, so beautiful, so *genuinely real*, that I can confidently say that none of us will forget it.

There was beautiful classical Indian music in what appeared to be a centuries-old stable or barn of some sort, with locals dressed in their finest *sarees* (women) and *dhotis* (men), singing along and dancing. There were twenty caparisoned elephants decked out in jewels and necklaces and bells that rivaled the collection of any Santa Barbara socialite. (Clarification: I am not likening any Santa Barbara socialites to bejeweled elephants; I meant only to communicate the beauty of the elephants and their appointments.) There was fire and drumming and there were royals and peasants and holy men, all walking together, barefoot in the sand and dirt, artfully dodging fresh mounds of elephant dung while trying to get as close to the magnificent beasts as possible to pray and show their dedication.

It was sweltering, hot with a ton of humidity, and the people were packed tightly together, soaked with sweat, and yet they laughed and talked and played and held hands with the kids on their shoulders and the elders and dizzying crowd around them.

And there we were, the Mazzas from Santa Barbara, right in the middle of the whole thing, sweating, shaking hands and laughing and talking about California and our kids—Lily and Kate continue to be a huge draw here—and our house and my profession and who knows what else.

The hours flew by and we left late, stopping only on the advice of Vishnu, our rickshaw driver-turned-guide-turned-friend, for some cauliflower fried in a red paste on the street and a lime and sugar-cane drink to wash it down before heading back to Fort Kochi over countless bridges and moonlit country roads in the open air.

I will miss India but will always hold it close, ready to be recalled, vividly, ready to be savored again and again.

It has been truly unforgettable.

CHAPTER 31
(FAMILY) MAN TIME

Soppong, Thailand
December 2011

Macho, macho man.
—The Village People

WE'RE IN NORTHERN THAILAND, have been for almost two weeks. We started in Chiang Mai (loved it) and then headed northwest in a spiffed-up minivan toward the Thai/ Burmese border, stopping and hanging out in Pai—a little hippie enclave that we seriously dug—and then moving on (in a far less spiffy minivan) to Soppong and a very cool little cabin out in the jungle on some pristine river very near the aforementioned border, deep in opium country.

Now I could spend the next few thousand words telling you all about the wonderful cities and amazing temples we've visited, the delicious food and drink we've gobbled and guzzled (respectively) and the gorgeous geography we've crisscrossed recently. I could tell you all about what a fantastic time we're having. And it would all be true.

But I'm not in the mood to talk about that stuff. There's an issue that's affecting my *performance*, for lack of a better word. I'm feeling a little *dysfunctional*, I guess.

I'm just not myself.

I went back and re-read a bunch of recent writings, you see, and I couldn't help but notice the overwhelmingly effeminate tack I've been on for some time now. I mean *spa days* and *yoga*? Near constant references to peace and love? I've even come across pictures of me galloping down a beach on the back of a white Arabian stallion. (I'd had a few cocktails before I got on that horse so it's not as bad as it sounds, but still.) The whole thing is bordering on completely ridiculous.

I put quite a bit of thought into this, and my feeling, my *self-diagnosis*, if you will, is that I am suffering from a short term psychosis stemming from the fact that I have spent every day—every single damned day—of the past six months surrounded by three (often particularly *girly*) women. I mean, we haven't even had two rooms since *Vic Bay* in South Africa. That was a long time ago, man, a real long time ago.

My own daughters now often refer to me as their *"fuzzy little chubby man."* (I couldn't make that up.) When we play family games of Uno or Trouble or whatever, they all—my previously supportive wife included—gang up on me and do everything possible to prevent me from winning, teasing me relentlessly the whole time ("it's *girls* against *boys* daddy, and you're the only *boy* and *you're a fuzzy little chubby man*...ha ha ha ha, etc.).

It's mental abuse, I tell you. *Mental abuse.*

And now that they've softened me up psychologically, they've started in on the physical stuff. It's happening all the time lately. There's a new "game" the kids "play," and it involves waking me up each morning by repeatedly jumping on my (tired) back, screaming, "1, 2, 3, 4, who's knocking on your door?!" Wendi just watches and laughs—cackles, I tell you—and does nothing to protect me from my tiny, merciless tormenters.

They're plain beating me up. And it's really starting to take a toll. I'm starting to show some significant wear and tear. My heretofore rugged masculinity is starting to suffer. Badly.

But, alas, my condition is not terminal. It is quite curable, in fact, with a steady regimen of something best described by two simple words. Two simple, beautiful words.

MAN TIME.

There are as many names for this phenomenon as there are groups of males in the world, and it has been around since the dawn of time. I once knew it, many years ago, as a BRO OUT, but over the years it has developed, and rightfully so, into MAN TIME and I will use this moniker to describe that which every one of us knows by one name or another.

Incidentally, I cannot personally take credit for this particular term. It comes from a friend. Let's call him "B-Dog," for convenience. B-Dog likes his MAN TIME. Now saddled—I'd say "blessed" here but, hey, it's MAN TIME so I can't be bothered—with a wife and children, he is all the more likely to need some time on the golf course with a prodigious amount of scotch or whiskey and a cigar.

That reminds me of an old MAN TIME classic. Me and B-Dog (yeah, I know, but grammatical precision is disfavored during MAN TIME) spent a long morning drinking and gambling—oh, sorry, I mean golfing—a few years back up at *Sea Ranch* and secretly decided to continue the debauchery at a nearby watering hole before heading back to our wives at the cabin. Everything was going splendidly, right up until B-Dog's wife *actually called the bar*—there was only one in town—and ordered us home like two busted teenagers.

She and Wendi spent the rest of the day at a spa, sipping Chardonnay and relaxing while me and B-Dog (again, I know) worked hard on a big, romantic "We're sorry for acting like drunken children" dinner. Fantastic.

Back to Thailand. I explained my present condition to Wendi in great detail one evening in Chiang Mai and suggested a treatment plan. "Ok, you can go down to the bar," she said with a sigh, eyes rolling clear back in her head. "But don't be too late."

So I helped get the kids to bed (quickly) and headed down.

It was perfect. There was a rough-and-tumble English Premier League match on and a raucous international (and predominantly male) crowd drinking large *Singhas* by the dozen in a simple little open-air place decorated by colored Christmas lights. (You've seen this place in every movie ever written that has a scene depicting a southeast Asian bar.) I found a spot near the television and joined in.

I was feeling better by the minute.

The match ended and nearly everybody dispersed to other points in the city. I stayed to finish my drink and was pleasantly surprised when a Thai guy with an acoustic guitar emerged from the back, smiling, and approached the stage.

"One song," I thought, *"I need to finish my beer anyway."*

He led off his set with a truly moving performance of Lionel Richie's classic, *Hello*. He knew very few of the lyrics but he mumbled and sang with infectious passion—he'd actually whisper the song's one-word title in an emotionally-tortured breathy sigh at appropriate intervals—and had real chops on the guitar.

Not exactly MAN TIME music, but I ordered another beer anyway.

He continued on for an hour or so, perhaps predictably mixing some Bryan Adams (*Everything I Do*) with Pink Floyd (*Wish You Were Here*), Rick Springfield (*Jessie's Girl*) and Eric Clapton (*Wonderful Tonight*). Incidentally, the only person I know who would have enjoyed that set as much as I did is my wife, and I lamented the fact that she wasn't sitting beside me, even despite the fact that this was technically MAN TIME.

I felt rejuvenated when I woke up in the morning but couldn't help feeling like I had been shortchanged with the romantic acoustic guitarist knocking out love ballads from an era gone by.

As I was laying in bed considering the whole thing, the children launched a genuinely clandestine attack that included amplified emotional and physical abuse. Relentless teasing and laughing and jumping on my back and calling me their "dog" and all sorts of terrible things I can't possibly mention here.

It was total humiliation at the hands of my small but surprisingly strong and agile persecutors, all as my wife sat idly by, pretending that everything was fine.

Pretending not to hear my desperate cries for help.

I needed more MAN TIME, better quality MAN TIME, and I needed it right away. It turned out that I was in the right place for it.

We'd had dinner a couple nights earlier with some friends from Santa Barbara who happened to be in Thailand (we had a great time together at a restaurant at the base of a waterfall), and had discussed seeing a *Muay Thai* fight—a particularly brutal form of organized combat—while in Chiang Mai.

It was just what I needed. I talked to Wendi. Arrangements were made.

We ended up with ringside seats for a night of eight fights. And even though most of the fighters were under twenty years old, it was a very fun time. The fights were entertaining, with near constant traditional *sarama* music—which consisted of a couple oboes and Thai drums and symbols (think up-tempo snake charmer music with serious percussion)—designed to encourage the contestants to keep at each other (and the crowd to keep drinking, I think). I made a few wagers with unscrupulous local Thai folks without success. (I'm pretty sure that the fix was in; the fights were genuine but there was little threat of knock-outs given the relatively small size of the fighters, so the outcomes may have been, um, divined by some of the locals, especially the ones that liked to gamble with foreigners.)

I had a great time and woke Wendi up to tell her all about it when I got back to the apartment. "Does that mean you're cured?" she asked tiredly.

"I don't know," I said, let's wait to see whether the symptoms recede tomorrow."

I woke up feeling great (except for that darn headache from both the *Singhas* and the *sarama* music). I felt better, more ... *myself*. Sort of John Wayne meets Clint Eastwood and Chuck Norris. With that said, I wasn't all the way back.

More MAN TIME was in order, I was sure of it.

And then, as I laughed with my wife and kids over a lovely Thai breakfast of rice soup with pork, a funny thing happened. I couldn't shake the feeling that I wanted to bring them in on the secret pleasures of MAN TIME. It had just been too much fun to keep all to myself, and the whole point of our adventure is to be together and have some fun.

So we decided to rent a motorcycle and go fishing.

That's about as deep as you can get into MAN TIME.

Bueng Pai Farm is a wonderful little oasis a few kilometers outside of Pai in northern Thailand, and it has a bunch of bamboo bungalows set right on a beautiful man-made pond amongst all sorts of tropical vegetation in the middle of acres and acres of rice fields. The pond is stocked with monster catfish for some catch-and-release fun. And it takes a motorcycle—ok, a scooter—to get there.

Basically a MAN TIME double bonus.

With my wife and kids to boot.

First and most importantly, we taught the girls to fish, and they really enjoyed it. And I thoroughly enjoyed dozens of sinister moments luring them in close with gentle language and empty promises to examine one gigantic (and horrifyingly ugly) catfish after another. When they'd get close, I'd go quiet and let them start to reach out to touch the beast, then I would scream and chase them around with the damned thing, yelling about how it was attacking and biting and doing all sorts of bad stuff.

Payback, my friends, is a bitch.

Run and Orn, the proprietors of *Beung Pai*, are wonderful people, warm and hospitable in a decidedly Thai fashion. They proudly make delicious slow-cooked meals from the organic garden at the farm and offer a very well-equipped and comfortable kitchen for all guests to use (as well as free herbs and vegetables and fruits from the property).

We fished and ate a lot during our four days and nights at *Bueng Pai*. (Wendi and I even stayed up late one night fishing from our little deck on the pond under a full moon.) And we explored Pai on the scooter—yes, all four of us squeezed on to one small scooter, India-style, much to the amusement of the locals—enjoying the nightly street markets and food and music and art scene and everything else that makes Pai such a special place. (We liked it so much that we are actually heading back for a few more nights. Fantastic spot.)

Perhaps best of all was the fact that I emerged cured. It was a remarkable recovery.

"I'm glad you're back to yourself," Wendi said (playfully) on our last night at *Bueng Pai*. "Funny that it took fishing with a bunch of girls to rid you of the psychosis you told me had been caused by a bunch of girls in the first place."

"Yeah, thanks babe."

"Maybe you and B-Dog should start calling it FAMILY MAN TIME instead of just plain old MAN TIME."

Maybe she's on to something there, I thought, and made a suggestion.

And that was how we decided (on the spur of the moment) to head up to a place we'd heard of called *Cave Lodge*. It's basically a bunch of cabins in the Thai jungle near the Burmese border that are surrounded by beautiful rivers and waterfalls and huge caves and other geographic wonders. We've been here a few days and are doing all sorts of manly things—cave exploration, jungle hikes, ping pong, etc. It's great, another fantastic little place that is a bit off the beaten path.

I feel terrific. You know, back to myself. Sort of John Wayne meets Clint Eastwood and Chuck Norris.

And maybe Bill Cosby.

The truth is that we've had a marvelous time up in northern Thailand. Chiang Mai is really beautiful and wonderful. We've had lots of family foot massages—Lily and Kate absolutely love them—and great food in street markets. We've seen beautiful sights and generally hung out and had a lot of fun. We even took a terrific Thai cooking class together that we'll surely bring home with us when (if) we return.

Anyway, peace and love.

No! That's not right. Let me try that one again.

MAN TIME.

(Yeah, that's better.)

CHAPTER 32
A CHRISTMAS STORY

Pai, Thailand
December 2011

You'll shoot your eye out, kid.
—Santa Claus

"But how is Santa going to find us, *Daddy*?"

It was a reasonable question given the circumstances.

Both of them looked up at me sheepishly, with a certain innocent desperation that perhaps only exists in little girls wearing pajamas and getting ready for bed. Sort of sad puppy dog meets *Cindy Lou Who*. I had to think fast.

"Well, girls, we'll send him a letter. Just like we do back in California."

"But *Daddy*," Lily carefully considered, "you keep saying that we are in the middle of the jungle in Thailand." (Damn that homeschooling.) "How will he get it?"

I was a litigator for some fairly sophisticated clients for a good number of years, effectively trained to think clearly and remain calm on my feet while under pressure. But we've been traveling for six months now and I'm emphatically not in what you might call top form.

So I panicked.

"Don't worry you guys," I stammered, "Mommy and I will figure something out."

Lily was right, of course. We'd been staying at the *Cave Lodge* outside of Soppong in the Thai jungle near the Burmese border for a few days. Christmas was just a week away. There was no post office, no messenger service, no meaningful way to communicate with the outside world. And email just doesn't work for something like this. (Imagine the barrage of questions from a hostile gang of tech-savvy and inquisitive six and four year old girls: "Why hasn't he responded, *Daddy*?" or "How did you get his email address, *Daddy*?" or "Why don't we just Skype him, *Daddy*, like we do with Grandma and Papa?" I may not be in top form, but I'm not walking into that one.)

Incidentally, the *Cave Lodge* is a fantastic place. On the outskirts of a remote Thai village and surrounded by beautiful country and a host of caves, it is a backpacker-type place consisting of a series of huts on the *Lang River* and a lodge that provides a nice place to relax and simple but tasty food and drink. There's extensive kayaking, trekking and (not surprisingly) caving, and Aussie-owner John Spies is very connected and knowledgeable, having lived in and extensively explored the area for nearly three decades. John and his wife are also great hosts, quick with tall tales about their many (wild) years building and running the *Cave Lodge*.

We spent one day on a bamboo raft floating through *Tham Lod* ("Through Cave") and stopping with our guide to explore the inner sanctums of what is a massive and frankly stunning cave network. The river is teeming with fish and was a real hit with the kids.

The same evening, we watched several hundred thousand swallows circle lower and lower in the sky, finally flying at mach speed into *Tham Lod* at sunset—pretty incredible—and then hiked back through the jungle to the lodge in the oily darkness. Another day we set ourselves up on a secluded rocky river beach on the *Lang* and read and talked and played in the water. (Then we treated ourselves to a rustic but fantastic herbal sauna.)

Simple and a real treat for all of us.

Wendi and I stayed up late one night on our creaky porch, listening to the river and the sounds of the jungle and staring at a close moon and bright stars. We hadn't talked for some time when a couple *Kongming lanterns—aka* "sky lanterns," effectively mini-hot air balloons constructed from rice paper and wire (for those of you with young kids, think of the floating lights in *Tangled*)—drifted into view downriver. They glowed brilliantly against the night sky.

We turned to each other and smiled.

It turns out that my wife and I think quite a bit alike.

The next day, Lily and Kate wrote their note to Santa. That night, just before bed, we stood on the bank of the river with our very own sky lantern lit and ready for takeoff, waiting for a shift in the warm and gentle breeze. When it came, we made a wish and watched as our lantern floated north, burning brightly, with the handwritten dreams of two little girls securely fastened inside.

Merry Christmas and happy holidays to everybody.

CHAPTER 33
SLOW BOAT ON THE MEKONG

Luang Prabang, Laos
December 2011

---

*There's no earthly way of knowing which direction
we are going.
There's no knowing where we're rowing or which way
the river's flowing.
Is it raining? Is it snowing? Is a hurricane a-blowing?
Not a speck of light is showing so the danger must be growing.
Are the fires of hell a-glowing? Is the grisly reaper mowing?
Yes, the danger must be growing 'cause the rowers
keep on rowing.
And they're certainly not showing any signs
that they are slowing.*
—Willy Wonka

I HAVEN'T BEEN ENTIRELY HONEST over the past month.
And, given the proximity of the New Year and my intended resolutions of generally high(er) ethical and moral standards, I thought I'd take this opportunity to come clean, you know, to start 2012 off on the right foot.

So here it is: This whole extended family travel thing is not all Thai cooking classes and sky lanterns of dreams. It's not all romance in France and passion in Italy. There are hard times, too, and they often involve the challenges associated with the actual *travel* portion of our travels.

The getting hither and yon, you know, the logistics of the whole operation.

There is perhaps no single better example of these challenges than our recent voyage to Laos. We were relaxing in wonderful Pai (again), when we decided that it sounded fun to spend Christmas in Luang Prabang—another (allegedly) wonderful little town, this one in northern Laos. There are many ways to get to Luang Prabang from Pai and we very nearly just flew but ultimately decided that we wanted the experience of reaching the former French colonial village in a more traditional way.

So we reserved a few seats on the "slow boat" that meanders down the *Mekong River* for two days from Chiang Khong on the Thai border to our chosen destination. (There is, logically, a "fast boat" that does the same trip in a single day but that boat requires helmets and executed waivers and we were repeatedly warned against it. "Slow" is pretty much our scene at this point, anyway.)

The first hurdle we faced was just getting to Chiang Khong. That involved a seven-hour minibus tour of hell, taking us over towering spires of rock and jungle on the windiest and arguably most dangerous roads we've ever seen (including in Nepal and India) as our driver made incrementally more aggressive passes that often bordered on suicidal. No guard rails, potholed or nonexistent pavement, steep ascents and descents at high speed and hundreds of hairpin turns and switchbacks ... all night long.

We got into Chiang Kong at 3:30 am with daughters who resembled the undead far more than little girls. (At least they slept the whole time, even if it was Dramamine induced;

neither Wendi nor I got as much as a moment of shut eye, opting instead to exchange frequent wide-eyed stares as we watched yet another life threatening scene unfold in front of us.)

Chiang Khong is a Thai border town. The accommodation was, consequently, less than spectacular. Let me put it to you this way: We "slept" (read: tossed and turned) in two single beds for a couple hours in all of our clothes. It was freezing, the windows wouldn't close and cleanliness was not a top priority. I will spare you the details but multiply whatever you're thinking by, say, ten and you will get a feel.

The next morning was consumed with crossing the border into Laos. We've dealt with interesting immigration and visa issues in lots of places at this point but crossing the *Mekong* and getting into Lao territory was an entirely new cup of tea. A long, patience-testing morning devolved into an all out mad rush on an open-air Laotian visa-on-arrival counter that was being bombarded from every side. The place was essentially the gladiator arena of foreign entry points, a real global crossroads that pitted, say, seasoned Spanish backpackers against English nobles or, in our case, a smiling American family against weathered Thai construction workers.

It was quite a scene.

We finally made it to the ridiculously long and rectangular slow boat and found our seats (not bad). But as we got ourselves situated (this takes longer than you think with the kids and books and games and food and drink etc.), a German man in his fifties stepped onto the boat and promptly fell into the totally unmarked and gaping hole in the floor through which our bigger bags had passed into a below-deck storage area just a moment before. (His ego was battered but he was otherwise peachy. And very lucky.) We counted three others who nearly met the same fate but were rescued by fellow passengers. I think that the crew was actually taking bets on who might tumble the whole time.

We spent the next six hours flying down the *Mekong*—"slow boat" is a relative term, apparently, that stems from a comparison to the deadly "fast boats" that kept speeding by with unhappy helmeted passengers holding on for dear life—with a Lao man in old US ARMY embroidered fatigues holding an intimidating M16 at our feet and a host of chickens clucking away on the roof above our heads. When our machine gun-toting neighbor saw the children he reluctantly removed the clip from his military grade weapon and smiled shyly.

We spent the night in a decent accommodation (our standards are not exactly what they were when we left Santa Barbara) in a fairly seedy Lao frontier town called Pak Beng and woke early to make the boat on time.

And then we spent the next nine or ten hours doing the same damned thing.

Here's the kicker: We loved every minute of it. All of us. We read and played games and enjoyed the indisputably gorgeous vistas of the *Mekong River Valley* and laughed and talked with the travelers and locals around us. We drank tea and had treats (sodas and chips and suckers). And an old Lao woman at the back of the boat was even selling singles from a fully stocked cooler of ice cold *BeerLao*, which just may be the best drop we've had to date. It was great.

So the cat is out of the bag. It's not all sunshine and butterflies and cooking classes all the time. There are challenges. There are hardships.

But we take them in stride and keep smiles on our

faces and springs in our steps. We wouldn't start the New Year any other way.

Happiness, health and prosperity in 2012.

To everybody.

CHAPTER 34
BUDGET CRISIS

Bangkok, Thailand
December 2011

One night in Bangkok makes a hard man humble.
—Murray Head

ONCE UPON A TIME, many moons ago, my wife and I secretly huddled around our dinner table with a dozen freshly sharpened number two pencils stuffed into our respective pocket protectors, a new pad of graph paper straight from tenth grade trig spread out before us and Wendi's ancient Texas Instruments calculator at the ready. We rolled up our sleeves.

And we dug in.

We roughed up some numbers, baby, and came up with a budget—a very vague, ambiguous and nebulous budget—for our travels.

This was groundbreaking for us, frankly. We never really had a "budget" before then. Sure, we were "financially responsible" to a degree, funding IRAs and 401(k)s for ourselves and 529 plans for the kids. We had (and have) no debt beyond some left over law school tuition. But despite being pretty clean, we never thought much about (seemingly dreadful) "budgeting."

We just did our best to live within our means and enjoy what was a comfortable life for us.

It turns out that these are not hallmarks of effective budgeters. So it is perhaps not particularly surprising that our late night number crunching was basically a waste of time; we pretty much ignored the purported "budget" from the word go.

It all started innocently enough. A cute little farm-house out in west County Cork that was a bit more expensive than the accommodation numbers allowed. A comfortable apartment on the Left Bank in Paris's (aristocratic) 7th Arrondissement. A week-long self-guided boat trip on the canals in Burgundy.

A few indulgences, if you will, all for the kids' enjoyment, of course.

Then there was the week at *Riva degli Etruschi*, the Italian family resort on the Tuscan Coast that was so fun, so non-touristy, so darn *Italian*, that is was worth each and every extra dime. Oh, and the great bottle of sparkly pink wine we savored in the afternoon sun on the *Canal Grande* in celebration of finding Kate after we'd lost her in Venice earlier that morning. The quick flight from Istanbul to central Turkey and back to experience the wonder that is Cappadocia. (That reminds me, there was a truly fantastic dinner with some great California friends in an Istanbul fish market that involved delicious Turkish grub and a considerable amount of top-shelf Turkish *Raki*. Definitely not in the budget.) The oceanfront places on *Vic Bay* and *J-Bay* in South Africa, ensuring quick beach and surf access. Too much *Chenin Blanc* at *Spier Winery* in Franshhoek and the consequent "Cheetah Experience" that probably endangered the lives of our children.

The list goes on and on.

None of these things have been extravagant, mind you,

just comfortable and a lot of fun. We would do it all again, just as we have this time around, even despite the fact that our trip is surely a bit shorter than it would have been had we stuck to the numbers and eaten only butter—oh, excuse me, *buerre*—and jam on baguettes the entire time we were in France. But, hey, what fun is that? (And it turns out that Lily loves *rillettes* and Wendi hates *andouillette* sausages. Who'd have known but for a few trial and error sessions in decent French cafes?)

Wendi and I have both known of our excesses for some time now and recently firmly agreed to curb them in favor of a more disciplined approach. "We're adults, for crying out loud," we said, convinced of our resolve, "we can impose and stick to some reasonable limits. We can control our sometimes childlike impulsive behavior." We even shook on it.

But a few nights ago in Bangkok, well, oops.

We did it again.

We couldn't help it. We'd just come off a week in Laos (which was great, truly, but had its challenges) and had one night in the Thai capital in the middle of a two-leg flight to Indonesia. We thought we'd spend a whirlwind afternoon and night exploring a city that we've heard quite a bit about. But when we got to the *JW Marriott Hotel Bangkok* (the *"J-dub"* to us), all of our plans flew straight out the view window in our sixteenth floor suite.

We stretched out on the luxurious bed (Wendi and I had it to ourselves!); we each showered for hours with an endless supply of hot water; we ordered room service (lots of it); we lounged by the pool. Wendi and I both worked out and took long saunas and steams and cleaned up in the locker room. (Wendi actually felt like "a girl again," she said, grateful for the chance to clean up and pamper herself.) We watched CNN on a flat screen television. We slept late.

We never left. We didn't see a damned thing in Bangkok.
But we'll never forget our night at the *J-dub*.
Even if it didn't exactly pencil out in the budget.

PART THREE

STARTING OVER

I want to take the preconceived
out from underneath your feet;
We could shake it off and instead
we'll plant some seeds.
—Jack Johnson

CHAPTER 35
COMING CLEAN

Ubud, Bali
Indonesia
January 2012

More important, I've also learned that if you've got a dream,
you have to try it;
you must get it out of your system.
You will never get another chance.
If you want to change your life, do it.
—Jim Rogers, *Investment Biker*

I'M A FAIRLY EMOTIONAL GUY, quick to laugh or cry and often driven, at least initially, by nothing more than enthusiastic optimism and my gut. I've always loved trying new things and taking on what many would call at least some risk, although I tend to focus on upside potential rather than downside and thus think of most new things as opportunities rather than risky propositions (see what I mean by enthusiastic optimism?). It's just who I am, for better or worse; I have long since stopped trying to be someone or something else.

I think, though I'm not totally sure, that my wife actually sees these as *good* qualities. (What can I say? I married well.) And I know, after more than sixteen years—our first date was

December 27, 1995, at *Café Tiramisu* on Belden Place in San Francisco—that she likes a little adventure and mystery and is pretty much always ready for anything (though she won't always admit it). She is also incredibly balanced and mellow, which helps stabilize my bipolar tendencies in times of great internal angst. All of this has resulted in what I consider a uniquely strong friendship and happy marriage, one for which I am truly grateful.

One that I love dearly.

All of this has served us well over the years. We've done a lot of very fun stuff, memorable stuff, that maybe we wouldn't have done had we been unwilling or unable to make some tough decisions. Packing everything into a shipping container and spending seven months traveling with the kids is just one example. Quitting a relatively lucrative job with a respected law firm in San Francisco to move to Santa Barbara (with a pending pregnancy and a young daughter) comes to mind as another. There are many.

It's been an interesting road, my friends. A good road.

But, alas, I digress. Given my aforementioned emotional disposition, it is perhaps not surprising that I found myself in tears on New Years' Eve as I watched Wendi and the girls take a traditional Balinese dance class in Ubud, hibiscus in their braided hair and long tight colorful wraps around their legs. They were smiling and laughing and dancing to beautiful Balinese music, genuinely happy.

I was literally overcome with love for them.

And as I sat there, it hit me that this trip, this uninterrupted time with my wife and daughters, this freedom from the distractions and general bullshit of the sometimes mundane day-to-day existence of the business litigator, has been the best experience of my entire life. Far and away, hands down, no contest. I've loved every single minute of it.

The tears began to flow more freely as I came face to face with the simple fact that it is over.

———•———

Life is funny, man. It's unpredictable.

I mean, if, on Christmas morning, 2010, you told me that my wife and kids and I would take a two-day boat trip down the *Mekong River* from Thailand to spend a lazy week in northern Laos for Christmas 2011, relaxing in small French cafes in Luang Prabang, riding bikes by the *Mekong* and its confluence with the *Khan River*, exploring gorgeous waterfalls in the Lao jungle, seeing Lao ballet on Christmas Eve and feeding Buddhist monks in the ancient *Tak Bat* ritual early on Christmas morning, I'd have called you a lunatic. Straight up.

And if you had told me one month ago that we would have plane tickets from Bali to Denver—yeah, *Denver*—on January 17, 2012, I'd have had the same reaction.

But it turns out that both are true.

Let me start by saying this: We are still having a good time and are not totally ready to be coming home yet. I think it is fair to say that we truly love our present lifestyle in many important ways. In fact, we fully intended to end our trip in New Zealand up until very recently. But circumstances—and a pushy, belligerent Malaysian Air ticketing manager who wouldn't let us board our flight to Bali without a ticket off the island due to purported (and totally incorrect) visa-on-arrival requirements—led us to the current state of affairs.

We were initially quite torn but have since grown very comfortable with the decision we made in a flash—it is economically and practically prudent for lots of reasons, at least some of which are set forth below. (Wow. Did I just say "economically and practically prudent?" I'd better slow down and consider what I'm writing.)

The truth is that we are indeed growing tired of rifling through guidebooks and travel websites after the kids go to sleep and planning next moves (definitely) and living out of bags (sort of, but not as much as you'd think). Money is starting to run a bit low (though not too low to keep going for another month or two). We're a bit jaded, I think, and don't greet every new place with the same *joie de vivre* that we did back in June.

We miss random things that we always took completely for granted. Beds for the kids (we've pretty much shared one or two beds for months now), our coffee machine and just sitting back on the couch next to a fire at home all come to mind.

We miss Bucky the dog (though he has been very well cared for by my father and his wife in Colorado—that's why we're flying to Denver—and will probably be reluctant to leave with us for a two or three day drive to California in a rental car).

And we long ago made a deal that we wouldn't just keep going for the sake of being gone an extra month or two. We don't want to spend the last weeks of our time pinching pennies or wandering about listlessly. We want only the great memories we already have, not some bittersweet conflicted ones that are just tossed in for longevities' sake at the end.

In short, we have what we wanted when we left: We are happy and mellow and focused on what we believe to be important. What else is there?

Now for the harder part.

This part of the story actually starts twenty-one years ago, when I got my first job at a small restaurant in Santa Rosa called Checkers. I ended up working there for around three years, progressing from busboy (ok, I washed dishes once or twice) to waiter and even to what I thought proudly of as a low-level management position of sorts. (By that I mean only that I closed the restaurant late at night as a seventeen-year old punk and handled money and nightly reports; the responsibility was good for me, so was the trust and confidence that was shown in me.) It was a pretty damn good job for a kid for lots of reasons, and I learned lots of valuable things there that have stayed with me over the years, things that even worked their way into my law practice, from how I dealt with clients and adversaries to how I kept my office in an organized and clean manner for efficiency.

My time at Checkers led to nearly seven additional years of front-of-the-house restaurant work, often five or six nights a week, as I went through school and for a year or two thereafter. It was hard work, good work, and I generally remember it fondly (to be sure, I remember its difficulties, too).

Most important, however, is that fact I made a couple lifelong friends at Checkers. I long ago began considering Mark and Ron, who owned but have since sold the Santa Rosa Checkers, my family. They loaned me money when I needed it, they have provided insight and guidance when I had none and have generally been there for me over many years, even a few very difficult years. (I like to think that I have reciprocated in some ways, but I doubt I have.) They visited Santa Barbara and took Wendi and me out to terrific dinners when we were broke college kids on more than one occasion. Wendi and I spent New Years' Eve 2000 at a fantastic party at one of their restaurants. I popped the question one morning in their gorgeous guesthouse that Wendi and I have so many memories in. We had our rehearsal dinner in another of their restaurants and were married the next day amongst the vineyards at their ranch just outside of Calistoga in the Napa Valley.

They have employed just about every other person in my immediate family at one time or another, often when we needed it most. (My younger sister Kim was waiting tables at that New Years' Eve party, and we have the pictures to prove it. Classic. And Kim met Ryan in that very same restaurant many years ago; and Ryan is now both her husband and a close friend of mine.)

Lily peed all over Ron the first time they met, when she was maybe just a couple months old. Mark (both of them, really) taught me a lot about life—the important stuff—over the years. I think that is about all I can actually admit on the record. Let's just say that we've had our share of good times together over the past couple decades and leave it at that.

Mark and Ron have made a huge impact in my life, and my wife's, and we are lucky to count them amongst our closest and most meaningful friends.

And now, once again, they are making their presence felt.

We talked for years about how romantic, how totally cool, it would be to one day reunite and collaborate to do something together, something good. We fanaticized about my coming back, not as a busboy or waiter, but as someone who might someday help them at least quasi-retire and enjoy the fruits of their many years of hard labor in a difficult and unrelenting business, especially in the Napa Valley. We talked about my eventually coming and learning their trade, with them, from them, and using my background to complement and ultimately sheppard their business into a new era. About further growing the business they started so well all those years ago.

That time has come.

This is a very unique opportunity, an exciting one, one that doesn't come around all that often. Mark and Ron have crafted a successful group of four restaurants in Calistoga, California (the north end of the Napa Valley), and they have offered us the chance to take it into the future. This is something we cannot pass up; it could just be too damned *cool*.

The truth is that this is something we see as being just

what we want going forward, for lots of reasons. We see it as an opportunity to really integrate many of the things we've found out here on the road into our day to day life, perhaps more than if I were to return and simply go back to litigating. The timing is perfect: No job to quit, no home to move out of, no switching schools mid-year. And, as those of you who know me know, I have a real passion for all things food and wine and enjoy spending time around the table with friends and conversation. I hope to bring that passion, together with many of the things I learned as a lawyer and many of the things we've learned over the past months, to the business of restaurants.

We are confident that it will be a success. (There's that optimism again.)

So, it's an easy decision in many ways.

All we have to do is move to the Napa Valley.

And that should be easy too. The Valley is indisputably beautiful. Both Wendi and I grew up nearby and know the area well. There is plenty to do for kids and adults alike. We have lots of good friends all over northern California. Both of our families are close. San Francisco is just over an hour away. So is Marin. Tahoe. The Russian River. Bodega Bay and the north coast of California (something Wendi and I love very much). I can go on and on.

But the Valley is not Santa Barbara, and making the decision to move has been one of the hardest decisions we've ever made, if not the hardest. We made the decision to leave Mill Valley and our very good friends in Marin and northern California to move to Santa Barbara five years ago for some very good reasons. And the five years we've spent in SB were some of the best of our lives.

Everything was perfect, in many ways, and we are running from nothing. We agree that we wish we could come up with something negative about SB to make leaving easier, but we can't. At the end of the day, we leave reluctantly, even with the prospect of doing something that we anticipate will be very fulfilling.

For the first time in seven months, I don't really know what else to say.

We will miss you all very much.

And we look forward to buying you a great glass of wine each and every time you come through the Napa Valley.

You will always be family to us.

Life is funny, man. It's unpredictable.

I don't think we really understood it at the time, but we effectively turned our life over to near total unpredictability (fate?) when we packed our bags all those months ago. Maybe I said it best in *Thoughts of Home*, the first blog I wrote back in New Jersey in June 2011, after spending an evening catching fireflies with Lily and Kate and a enjoying a few glasses of a lovely French red over conversation with Aunt Bev and Uncle Mark and my cousins:

> *Yet now, as we begin our travels after months of planning and plotting and talking and thinking, it seems that nothing is really certain. From where we will go to when we'll come home and what we do when we get there. From how we will adapt to our newfound lifestyle as vagabond parents and gypsy spouses to how our kids will react as world citizens. From what each of us may ultimately get out of this to what each of us may not. These are uncertain times. Uncertain times indeed.*

We found the answers to many of those questions out here on the road. And I think we will find more in the Napa Valley.

Happy 2012 everybody.

We'll see you soon.

CHAPTER 36
THE HAPPIEST PLACE ON EARTH

Nusa Dua, Bali
Indonesia
January 2012

---

*Sorry, folks! We're closed for two weeks to clean and repair
America's favorite family fun park.
Sorry, uh-huh, uh-huh, uh-huh!*
—Marty Moose

WE'RE NOT IN BALI right now.

Oh, well, sure, if you were to look at a map, in an effort to accurately pinpoint our geographic location, for example, it would appear that we are indeed in *Nusa Dua* on the island's southern tip. Close to *Kuta* and *Uluwatu* and all the places you and—judging from the number of gaudy, gawking tourists presently around us—apparently every other person in the world has heard about. (In fact, many of them are staring at me even now as I sit alone, hunched over the keyboard in the darker corner near the baby grand in the lobby bar, trusty *Bintang* close at hand, typing furiously, then pausing to reconsider my typically exaggerated prose, then typing furiously again.) And you might well assume from your hypothetical review of our immediate longitude and latitude that we are indeed in Bali right now.

But we're definitely not in Bali right now.

We are in the Republic of Westin Resorts, a vast and geographically scattered ideological empire with key strategic installments around the globe, sort of like, say, *al-Qaeda*, I guess. And like *al-Qaeda*, the Republic is clearly bent on monotonous uniformity of thought and experience (aka brainwashing) and thus on stomping out all things authentic and good in each of its strongholds. It should be resisted, fought even, but our experience is that significant civilian lives would be at stake in any such battle.

Indeed, our reconnaissance efforts reflect that there are hordes of sunburned jet-setters strolling the lobbies and prowling the swim-up bars, eagerly displaying their vast wealth and power, proudly donning their finest leisure suits and resort wear and prancing about the perfectly manicured beaches in wedges and loafers and shiny bathing suits and see-through cover-ups and their fanciest *bling* like brightly colored bejeweled peacocks with tail-feathers spread wide and chests fully inflated. People who seem to not only accept but fully support the Republic and its ideals. People who don't really care where they are, instead focusing only upon whether there is a breakfast buffet that boasts everything from poached sea bass to filet mignon and an internet connection.

In short, the Republic is chalk full of my archest-enemies.

It must, therefore, be destroyed.

But, given the circumstances and the significant potential for loss of life, it is perhaps best, for now, anyway, that the resistance remains quiet, patient, until a better opportunity presents itself. Until the wool over the eyes of the many wears thin and the light of day begins to shine through, illuminating the wrongs that have been and are still being perpetrated by the Republic. Until the hearts and minds of the oppressed can be won without unnecessary bloodshed.

And so we wait, comrades. And so we wait.

—◦—

We *were* in Bali, of course. We landed in Denpasar a couple weeks ago and went straight to Ubud, where we spent our New Years' holiday participating in the Balinese dance class I talked a bit about in *Coming Clean* and seeing a brilliant shadow puppet play just before the calendar turned to 2012. (The girls really enjoyed a very classy moment of live theater that involved a beautiful, intricately carved shadow puppet, um, *breaking wind* very, ah, well, let's see, *powerfully*, thereby causing a shadow arrow to fly across the screen and kill the windy party's adversary in what seemed, up until that moment, to be a serious religious battle. Good stuff.)

There is a fair amount to do in Ubud beyond just strolling the streets in town and hanging out in little cafes and perusing the local shops. One day we wandered a monkey forest brimming with curious (aggressive?) little beasts who stole food and shiny objects from the unwary, another day we hung out at the very cool local public library (totally open air) and took a painting class and read books. We had a decent room overlooking a rice field. The Ubud market is fun for a day. We ate a good to very good meal of suckling pig at *Ibu Oka*—Ubud itself is famous for its *Babi Guling* and *Ibu Oka* is at least one of the well-known places (probably because of the Bali episode of Anthony Bourdain's *No Reservations*, which despite the passage of time remains my favorite show on TV; the guy is classic and so are his books). We enjoyed Ubud, overall. It was just fine, thank you.

Ok, all right. The truth is that our expectations for Ubud were sky high. We'd heard and read a lot about it and always really looked forward to getting there. But when we did, we found Ubud a bit too crowded and a bit too, well, *touristy* for our taste. (For the record, we are not holier-than-thou travelers who no longer consider ourselves mere tourists or anything like that; touristy is just an accurate description of the place.) It felt like you could have been in any one of a hundred towns in many ways. The shops felt less authentic. The people weren't as friendly. The restaurants were resorty (is that even a word?), with frankly pretty ridiculous constructions of what should have been simple dishes. Come to think of it, the whole place felt a bit like the food looked and tasted.

Constructed.

None of this is the town's fault, of course, it is just a place that we missed by a decade or two. The world has discovered Ubud—the whole island of Bali, really—and has changed it. Cleaned it up. Toned it down. Commercialized it. Probably bettered it in some ways; probably lessened it in others.

You know these kinds of places. It isn't that they aren't still fun and cool. It is just that they are totally dumbed-down for mass consumption. Frankly, I think we are very sensitive to that after just spending a couple months or more in Nepal and India and Thailand and Laos. Hell, even South Africa felt more edgy.

Maybe it was a case of expectations gone too far. Maybe it was being there for the holidays. Maybe it was the fact that we are getting near the end of our travels.

Maybe we are jaded.

Whatever. Ubud wasn't what we expected and while we had a good time, we were also a bit disappointed. (Maybe we'll just have to return someday and try it again.) I'm glad that it was the first time we felt that way since we hit the road.

We left Ubud sooner than we envisioned and headed for a far more rural area up in northwest Bali on some friends' recommendation. The five hour drive was absolutely stunning.

Huge views of jagged, craggy peaks and vibrant terraced rice fields backed by an endless blue expanse, every shade of green imaginable (and then some), dense jungle and gorgeous rivers (it is the rainy season here). More of what we expected in Bali. Fewer people, more tropical, more remote.

More ... *us*.

When we arrived at *Taman Sari*, we knew we'd gotten it right. It's a simple place, a quiet place far from everything else. There's a sleepy black sand beach with a few tired dive shops and a coral restoration project that makes for great snorkeling. There's a restaurant just off the sand that serves easy meals. Fishing seems to be the local industry.

We got lucky and had a private salt-water pool at our place, which was essentially a fantastic room in an open-air compound with ample outdoor area for relaxation amongst a beautiful tropical garden. We swam and played in the morning and evening sun and in the afternoon downpours, thunder and lightning all around us; we watched a few movies; we strolled the beach; we snorkeled. Wendi and I shared a few bottles of wine on the deck after the kids went to bed.

We chilled. We did a lot of family time, something we've gotten pretty good at and know well after all these months on the road.

It turns out that it's not fancy resorts or constant stuff to do or see that has made our trip special for us; it's the time in simple places without much happening that really stands out. The times when we just hung out and made up games in a pool or sat around and shot the breeze with our kids and each other for hours or walked around and smelled flowers or watched frogs or lizards for an afternoon or went to the laundry-mat or did workbooks and read or whatever.

That's what it's all about, man. That's the trick to digging travel with the kiddies. Let go a bit, take it slow, make it fun.

And we found that (again) at *Taman Sari*. We stayed for over a week, not wanting to leave, not doing much of anything.

It was fantastic.

(Jesus, am I really going back to work in a few weeks? Wow.)

———— · ————

And so, I admit, it is perhaps puzzling that we presently find ourselves at the Westin Resort at *Nusa Dua*. Oh, it's not as bad as I made it sound at the beginning. (Actually, I take that back. It's just as bad, maybe worse, than I made it sound. The Republic will fall!) But we are enjoying it. We consciously chose it, in fact, knowing full well what we were getting into.

The place was actually *ranked* as one of the best resorts in Indonesia for kids for Christ's sake, what did we expect?

It's just that we have spent exactly no time over the past seven months in any place remotely like this one (by design, of course). Our thinking was always that we wanted to expose Lily and Kate to the world in an authentic way as much as possible, and while we haven't always been perfect, we've done a pretty good job in that regard.

As we looked at places to stay on Bali, however, we decided that we would treat the kids to a really fun resort/clubby experience, sort of as a celebration of all we've done over the past months. We really had good intentions and honestly thought that the kids would love it.

And they dig it, no doubt. I mean, what's not to like about a kiddie breakfast buffet with all kinds of sweet, chocolaty cereals and doughnuts with frickin' M&Ms stuck to the top and pancakes with chocolate syrup and who knows what else? Who doesn't like free ice cream sundaes with every meal, and constant movie time at the kids club? And there's kiddie "fishing" and hotel tours and star gazing (when there's no rain) and there's waterslides and tons of other (screaming, spoiled, sugared-up, exhausted, misbehaved) kids and, well, I think I've said enough.

It's the happiest damned place on earth.

But here's the thing. Lily and Kate have dug *everything* we've done, truly, even despite the total absence of kids clubs and breakfasts that result in mandatory visits to dental hygienists. So the Westin has really not been anything too special for them. I actually think that this whole super-resort thing has been a bit overwhelming and ridiculous, and that the girls are ready for some more simple time like that at *Taman Sari*.

Truth be told (*gasp!*), I think they had more fun when they were just hanging with us and I was throwing them around in our pool or playing guitar for them.

It's funny, and I wouldn't have known it seven months ago, but that's what I hope the legacy of this trip turns out to be. We're a close little family after all this time, happy and very comfortable to just hang together and do little beyond enjoy each other. We don't really need kids clubs and waterslides and sugar highs (although, don't get me wrong, there is a place for all that).

After all this time, it turns out that all we need is each other, man. I know it, for sure, positively. I feel it and I'm living it every day. And that's *unbelievably* cool to me. It means infinitely more to me than all the stamps in our passports or anything else. It is something to be protected and nurtured and cherished.

And I won't sacrifice it for anything or anybody.

That said, I really must get going. *Free Willy* is playing at the kids club tonight and it's *Parents' Night Out* and there is a (faux) Japanese restaurant with a sushi bar and fresh *maguro* and a special on foofy sake drinks, including a bright red/orange "Ninja Sunrise" complete with paper umbrella and pineapple slice. I hear they even throw in some vodka-infused watermelon and mango if you can tell them what movie is playing tomorrow night for the kids.

I guess this place isn't all bad. Just one Ninja Sunrise can't possibly hurt the movement. The pool bar does look pretty comfortable too...

Honey, where's my linen suit and Italian loafers and your hair gel? Get your best transparent blouse and biggest watch and let's hit the club after dinner; that techno medley of *DeBarge* tunes (*Rhythm of the Night* and everything!) I heard when we walked by last night was awesome!

(Aaaahhhh! Must fight. Brainwashing strong... down with the Republic!)

CHAPTER 37
ANOTHER NEW BEGINNING

St. Helena, California
United States of America
February 2012

If I knew the way,
I would take you home.
—Jerry Garcia

IT'S BEEN ONE HELL OF A MONTH.

Just four short weeks ago, we sat happy on the beach at *Padang Padang*, sun warming our brown skin, bellies full of vegetable rice plates with beautifully grilled pork and fried eggs and ice cold *Bintangs* from *Made's Warung*. The world had become a simple place, one without worry or stress (or meaningful responsibility, frankly).

In fact, looking back through the kaleidoscopic lens of hindsight, the world had become everything I always wanted it to be, filled with boundless possibility and optimism and happy kids and a smiling wife and the time to sit back and take it all in, every moment, every nuance, every breath.

But, alas, I always knew, in some darkened, nearly forgotten corner of my mind, that we had constructed our pretty perfect reality. I always knew, somewhere, that it would end someday and that we would go home, that I would go back to work, back to busier days and planned nights out and auctions and play dates and soccer practice and everything else that makes the real world the real world.

And so, under sunny mid-January skies and with a light breeze coming off the Indian Ocean, we packed our few belongings into our travel-worn bags for the last time. And we boarded a plane from Indonesia to Japan to Seattle to Denver. And after nearly thirty five hours of airport food and cat naps on public benches, we landed in Colorado, tired and strung out from the road (in the words of the immortal Bob Seger).

And we hugged Bucky the dog—he'd been staying outside Denver while we were gone—and we drove him back to California in a rented Ford Explorer.

And we came home.

Well, sort of anyway. As promised, we actually did move to the Napa Valley to pursue that restaurant opportunity. And while we already miss Santa Barbara and all the people and familiarity of the place, Wendi and I have known for a long time that we share a passion for food and wine and sitting around a table with friends enjoying both over great conversation. That passion was really re-awakened in the cafés of Paris and Lyon (and Luang Prabang and many other places) and in the fields of organic farms in Tuscany and in the streets of Delhi and the rural northern areas of Thailand and countless other food crazy cultures we visited.

And so we decided to take a chance on something new.

Something that we believe will incorporate at least some of the truly wonderful things we found out there in the big world into our daily lives. Something that we believe will keep the spirit of our travels alive and well within us for a long (long) time.

Something fun and new and exciting.

We rented a cozy Victorian on Main Street in St. Helena, a small rural-but-sophisticated town in the heart of a global center for food and wine and, increasingly, design and art and other wonderful things. Lily and Kate have started school and we are meeting friendly families with kids eager to know who the new girls are. We are settling into a routine.

The mustard is in bloom, and vibrant greens and yellows dominate otherwise dormant vineyards. The food and wine are exquisite. It is a beautiful place.

We are happy here.

It's funny to think back and realize that we knew so little about how all this would turn out when we set off all those months ago. It was an amazing seven months, the best of my life, a time when I was able to step away with the most important people and realize dreams and gain new perspective on life and happiness and everything else.

If I had it to do all over again, I wouldn't change even one single thing.

We left it all behind, and we didn't just survive, we thrived, together, as a family. And we now begin this next chapter in our lives as we began the last, with renewed direction and focus.

And perhaps most importantly, with each other.

EPILOGUE

Santa Barbara, California
United States of America
December 2013

Wanna pack your bags, something small;
Take what you need and we disappear.
Without a trace we'll be gone, gone;
The moon and the stars can follow the car.
And then when we get to the ocean;
We gonna take a boat to the end of the world.
All the way to the end of the world.
—Dave Matthews

IT'S BEEN A LONG TIME since I wrote that last line—almost two years, in fact. I always meant to get this all together into a polished manuscript but, well, things kept happening. Things kept *changing*. And I just didn't feel that the whole damned saga had ended.

Until now.

Napa didn't work out. It was one of the biggest professional and personal disappointments of my life. Without going into it in too much detail, my general feeling is that it just wasn't a good fit, despite the romantic optimism shared by at least some of the participants, and there were probably broken promises on all sides. Regardless, at the end of the day, it wasn't to be for a huge number of reasons.

So it failed.

Sort of.

Life is unpredictable, as I've said, and when you open yourself up to new experiences and possibilities, that unpredictability only expands and evolves, taking on a life of its own.

We'd returned to Santa Barbara before formally moving to Napa, of course, to see old friends and gather our belongings. I had never actually met the publisher of the paper for which I'd been providing a weekly travel column since our time in South Africa—Skype and email worked just fine—so I stopped into his office unannounced to introduce myself and thank him for publishing my (often rambling) stuff.

We were fast friends, soon laughing and talking about funny travel anecdotes and expectations about each other. He'd followed the column and the blog very closely, so he knew much about me and my family.

Then a curious thing happened.

Before we parted ways, he suggested that I continue the column. "You're not done," he told me pointedly, "this next chapter is just as wild as the first." And so he persuaded me to write the experience of a lawyer-*cum*-family traveler-*cum*-Napa Valley restaurateur.

I quickly agreed without thinking much of it, although I can't quite tell you why as I sit here today. I didn't see writing as anything more than a hobby then, and writing my experience in the food and wine business seemed an interesting endeavor. I saw no reason to stop it, I guess, even despite the fact that I wasn't earning much money.

The truth, as I see it, is that writing—just as much as playing games like *Water Moose* with my kids and spending long evenings with my wife—had become a part of my existence, it had worked its way into my daily routine.

I *enjoyed* it. In fact, I enjoyed most everything about my life at that point.

Imagine that.

We ended up spending around six months in that terrific house on Main Street in St. Helena, and we very nearly stayed for good. The Napa lifestyle was pretty much what we thought it would be, and we had a terrific time living in and exploring the Valley. There really is a passion for great food and wine (and art and design and lots of other cool stuff) and we thought, after the restaurant project went belly up, that I could open a small country law practice that might support a mellowed existence, maybe, one that really fit with much of what we'd learned about ourselves during our time on the road.

But then that darned unpredictability reared its mysterious head again. My publisher friend back in Santa Barbara called one afternoon and invited me to lunch. He knew that the restaurant project had failed—I'd detailed the end in my column—and that we had considered returning home to Santa Barbara.

I accepted his invitation and made the drive south.

Just two days later, we were sitting in the back of some non-descript dive over sandwiches and cold beer. He was pitching a concept for a brand new publication, one that fit my writing style and focus, he said, one that we might start together, as Co-Founders and Co-Owners.

That was it. Wendi and I weighed all of our options (we did indeed have some opportunities in the Valley at that point) and decided that it was important to keep pushing forward rather than standing still or, worse yet, going backward. So, after the kids finished the school year out, we packed up and moved back to Santa Barbara, back to our friends and the beach and the old school district, and we got started on another new life. You know, the one in which I was actually paid something to write and serve as Editor-in-Chief of a weekly hyper-local publication.

It took months of planning, but the *Santa Barbara Sentinel* hit the racks on October 5, 2012. I won't ever forget that day. I actually cried when I saw thousands of copies of the first issue flying off the printing press.

In many ways, that particular moment was the culmination of all we'd set out to do back in June 2011. Even if we had no idea what we were getting ourselves into at the time.

The *Sentinel* has been a blast. Readership has grown, ad dollars have come. I've pumped out thousands and thousands of words. My partner and I have grown a fun product and business and friendship. Additional writing projects keep popping up. I've practiced some law to make ends meet but as my writing has required more time and effort, I've devoted less to lawyering.

And I'm still enjoying it. Every day.

Maybe it's because I'm home more—a lot more—than I was before and have a bit more time to jump on the trampoline with the kids or practice guitar with Lily or tickle Kate. Maybe it's because I can wave to Wendi down in the garden (next to the chicken coop!) from my office at the house. It certainly isn't because we have more money; we don't. We have decidedly less. And yet things just keep working out as we continue pushing forward into new and unexplored territories.

Funny how that goes.

The fact is that the past couple years have been terrific, filled with new experiences and risks and challenges and mistakes and failures and successes and, frankly, a lot of creativity and collaboration and laughter and fun.

I wouldn't change a single moment of any of it.

Much like our time on the road.

It's Christmastime.

And as I sit, again, in my familiar chair in my familiar office, writing these words, I'm reminded of relaxing in a festive café in Luang Prabang two years ago, typing leisurely, glass of French red table wine nearby, Wendi, Lily and Kate playing a game in the corner opposite me, ancient rented bikes parked out front on a well-decorated Christmassy street that I could probably still find if back in Laos.

I'm sad, for a moment, then nostalgic. I want that time, *that particular time* with my wife and kids, back. But I know that's impossible. The girls are older now. Things have changed. Our life is here, in this moment, in this place, with these people and these experiences.

With that said, not a day goes by without something—a comment, a picture, a person, a place—from our time on the road together coming up in conversation. The kids *do* remember. And they *were* affected, in a very positive way (educationally, emotionally and otherwise). They clearly understand, even now, what a special time it was.

And it was.

I could talk all about how we've incorporated so much from our travels (and even our time in Napa) into our day-to-day existence; we have and that's certainly an enduring legacy of our experience.

But that's not really the point and I won't do it.

Seize the moment, people, it's fleeting and you can't get it back once it's gone. Don't let life just pass you by, there's too much beauty and love and happiness out there to miss.

You just have to go find it.

AUTHOR'S NOTE

THIS DAMNED BOOK would have never seen the light of day but for the help and guidance of so many, and I owe everybody who pushed me forward a debt of gratitude (or more). With that said, though, there are a few folks I thought I'd mention specifically, since they were absolutely integral in getting my thoughts on our experience into a blog, on to a website, into a newspaper and, ultimately, into these pages in this particular form.

First and foremost, Tim Buckley and the entire Buckley/Montecito Journal family for bringing my columns and photos to print and ultimately welcoming me into their writing and publishing world (you're friends and mentors, all of you, and I truly can't say enough about how much you've meant to me); Grant Lepper and Porter Communication for talking me into doing the website in the first place, and then for setting it up and teaching my Luddite-self how to use it; Peter Lance for taking the time to explain the intricacies of the self-publishing/publishing on demand/epub world; Walton Mendelson for helping me navigate that world and designing the book from soup to nuts with great care and patience; and, although the whole thing was dedicated to them at the outset, my wife, Wendi, and daughters, Lily and Kate, who encouraged me to publish *this* book in *this* form—it's an honest look at both our experience and my writing, which, I think, improved over time. The progression is a cool thing to see…even if some of the early chapters could use a little work. (There, I said it!)

Finally, my mother, Lynn, and father, George, who sent me away, kicking and screaming, to Madrid as a high school exchange student all those years ago. The truth is that my first time living in Spain was perhaps the most formative experience of my young life, and instilled in me a powerful sense of curiosity and an unshakeable (even if rather inconvenient and impractical) wanderlust. I wouldn't trade either for anything.

———

Oh, if anybody is interested, please do go check out the old site. We have a (painfully long) slideshow of some of our favorite photos up and some other fun stuff if you want to have a look. It's all at www.towheadtravel.com.

Peace.

And thanks for reading.